Excuse Me

Officer

The Funny Side of British Policing

PC Andrew Hole

Excuse Me Officer

Foreword 4

The Police 13

Going to the dark side 36

Training 47

First Shift 68

Never Volunteer 78

Back on the Front Line 86

PDR 98

Operation 102

First Couple of Years 106

Downturn 113

Time for a Change 124

Government Cut's 140

Jumper 165

Final thought and 2011 Riots 172

Copyright 190

Foreword

What are the police actually here for? The dictionary definition for 'Police' is, "The governmental department charged with the regulation and control of the affairs of a community, now chiefly the department established to maintain order, enforce the law, and prevent and detect crime." In an ideal world all of that would be true. With government cuts, and less police officers - has put a strain on the service that police can offer. Police forces have had to look at ways to reduce overheads and be more innovative in regards to the way policing is undertaken. The Windsor report has led to many changes and a radical overhaul of many aspects of policing. Some say, too many changes all at once that has had an effect on morale.

With a reduced number of officers available on the street due to austerity measures, retirement and the time it takes to recruit and train replacements, adds to the strain on a stretched service. The current number of police officers is not far off being as low as in the 1980s.

There was a 3.4% (4,516) fall in police officer numbers up to March 2013.

This is why if you can predict where crimes will happen, then you can put what is left there for the night. The criminal however likes to ensure these predictions are more often than not are incorrect. With some form of mysterious X-Men type power, they have the ability to undertake crime in a completely different area to the one a police operation has been set up to catch them in. New software developed in the United States, called the PredPol program allows police to feed in crime data, from which it calculates and highlights 250-yard zones at particular risk and is already being used.

Being a modern police officer is all about customer service and customer satisfaction, we have our clients (offenders) and customers (victims). After ten years of pounding the beat and driving around in my little police car complete with flashing lights. I have seen many changes, the criminals themselves have changed very little, simply making use of the latest technologies to perform even more weird and wonderful crimes. We now have a deluge of social networking and auction site type crimes to deal with as well as the usual, burglary, theft, violence and sexual offences to deal with. We must not forget Britain's binge drinking culture that also takes up a vast amount of time especially on a Friday or Saturday night. The lovable rogues in their hoodies that take up another major slice in police time, after that we finally get to crime as most people perceive it to be. With burglary, theft, murder oh and Facebook, but more about that later…

I am just a police constable, nothing special – just one of the many thousands who want to do a good job and serve our local communities. Indeed the local community would see more of me if I was not buried knee deep in paperwork, some of which have to be done triplicate, although the move to more electronic based materials will negate and make the process easier. The police officer is truly societies 'meat in the sandwich'. Some would say we are abused by some members of the public, who tell us what we should be doing as their servants. At the same time some feel we are abused by elements of the government also telling us what we should be doing - whilst enduring the recent cuts, pay freezes and pension changes. The cuts to the frontline have caused a drop in service. One force reporting that in 2010 it was able to respond to 92% of immediate or emergency incidents, in 2012 this had dropped to 73%, simply due to falling frontline officer numbers.

It is now a difficult task to join the police force, with the rigorous application and assessments that are undertaken as part of the recruitment process. For every one police officer post there are around seven applicants. The application form is scored on ten questions that are graded A, B, C and D, four of these questions being based on what is called 'Core Competencies', they need a grade B overall to pass. If they have met the grade B criteria, applicants progress onto the next stage. A tough day at the SEARCH assessment centre where the minimum pass requirement is 50% and many forces now want 60%. This is followed by an interview, fitness test, medical and final vetting. Once accepted, they then undertake the Initial Police Learning and Development

Program (IPLDP) at a training school for around 18 weeks, before joining their tutor at the sharp end for another 10 weeks. Before a final stint at training school. In total it is two years before they have passed their probation and can be classed as substantive. The learning curve is a steep one, as the amount of information about law and procedures you have to carry around in your head is quite vast. Learning to deal with difficult people, whilst taking verbal and on the odd occasion physical abuse, is something else these new recruits have to deal with. They are the ones who have chosen to step up and be the protectors of the public, putting themselves in harms way to do so. The 'job' can put a strain on any relationship and I have seen many marriages end in divorce. My first girlfriend just after joining up called Gail, blew me away, then sailed off into the sunset - she got a job on a cruise ship. It was a bit of a whirlwind romance though as she never liked dating a police officer. When I asked why she liked me and not my job, she said, "All cops are full of it, they seem to think they are better than the rest of us – you're alright though."

As for those desperate to join the job, they now have to look forward to a lower starting salary of around £14.50 an hour as a student officer, for what is becoming a more complex and wide ranging role. The average lifespan of a new cop said to now be around five years, before they move into a different career. More, now seem to see being a police officer as an occupation as opposed to a career. Some of the younger members joining up, see it as a stepping stone that looks good on their CV. They enjoy their time serving the public, but seem to get itchy feet at five years. Those that pass the five year mark tend to stay in until retirement. Some moving into a training role towards the end of their career or after retiring.

For those new officers joining the frontline - they join a dedicated and professional group of people working all hours of the day and night 365 days a year. Giving up family and personal time to keep the streets safe and be there in a community's time of need. The immeasurable rewards are still there, such as being there to support the public in their time of need. Catching a criminal is a real buzz, one that is akin to the buzz of a sale for a salesperson. Getting these naughty people off the street is what pretty much all cop's join up to do - even if the public perception is they only get 10 minutes in jail before being released to re-offend. Police Forces themselves have managed to do an excellent job of managing very tight budgets even if some of those hard decisions have not been to everyone's liking.

In the ten years I have been on the frontline, I have seen it all – some things that are truly horrific and shocking it has nearly brought me to tears, some things that are so funny I have nearly wet myself. I am still proud to be a police officer and be able to make a difference no matter how small. Like any career being a police officer has its ups and downs; recent years have been difficult, along with many public services feeling the effects of the world recession. The government has had to make hard decisions to stop our economy spiralling out of control. This book is not intended to be a rant about the police force or the government. Just a funny reflection of one fictional police officer - leaving you to make up your own mind if a policeman's lot is really a hard one! The job I do along with my colleagues is a vital one, trying to push the never ending tide of crime back…

Like one night when I pulled over a car for having a rear light out. I went over and asked the driver to join me on the pavement. As he got out the car I noticed he put something in his mouth, thinking he was swallowing drugs I asked him ,"Did I just see you swallow something?"

"Yep, that was my birth control pill," said the driver.

"Birth control pill?"

"Yep, when I saw your blue flashing lights, I knew I was screwed."

The so called 'birth control pill' turned out to be nothing more than a polo mint. I later found out that it was an old cop joke and I had swallowed it hook line and sinker!

I apologise unreservedly for my bad spelling and poor grammar, along with the 50 pence I spent having the book proof read by a monkey at Chester Zoo. It may well be the worst book you will ever read or be about as funny as watching paint dry. I also appolgise in advance for the plagerised jokes, as sadly I don't have the brain power to conjure up any new material…so feel free to feel sorry for this little A Hole.

PC Andrew Hole

The Police

After ten hours of duty, which involved being a lazy cop, eating one too many doughnuts and a quick run through McDonald's drive thru, I made my way to the front door of the police station. I stepped out into the starry night, which had a cool breeze, although not too cool being late September. I made the short walk across the car park to my car to get home to Mrs Hole. Mrs Hole is always happy to have me home and to this day thinks I am completely bonkers to do what I do, to be put in dangerous situations and suffer various levels of abuse. Being married to PC Hole is not easy; I must be the grumpiest cop alive at times especially after a very long and demanding shift. Oh and then there is my slight gut problem, which can clear a police station quicker than a police officer in need of assistance. My bowel problem is aptly named the 'Death Fart' as these smell as if something has died. I have caused poor work colleagues sitting next to me in the police car to nearly throw up. Mrs Hole has banished me to the garden on more than one occasion…

I am sure Mrs Hole has called me A Hole on many, many occasions - as have a few of the naughty people I work with, although they call me PC A Hole. As lovely and glamorous as Mrs Hole is, she is a real loser, she has lost my police keys twice, warrant card once and on another occasion, my whole kit bag. I am sure Mrs Hole would lose her head if it was not already held on with Blu-Tack.

I must admit maybe some of my failed romances are on my tendency to be grumpy, I also have the punctuation of a five year old and grammar to be truly ashamed of. The upside is that most solicitors and the CPS are unable to read my statements, so very rarely bother to call me into court. PC Writewell usually gets the honours, although he loves going to court as it means a day of sitting around doing nothing, before being called to the stand, usually around 2:30pm. Then it's an hour of slight grilling and cross examination, before PC Writewell can get off home for his tea. Whilst at court PC Writewell knows he will not pick up any more paperwork or get sent to any scary jobs, like a few months ago, when he got sent to a theatre with reports that a ghost had been seen, and all the actors had got stage fright. The ghost turned out to be nothing more than a practical joke by a stage hand, who had been cruelly teased about the recent death of his cat that strangely liked lemons. The cat was a real sour puss though.

Police officers are professionals up there with doctors, teachers and dentists. Although dentists seem to just empty my wallet as well as my mouth.

The police have two friends that help us out on occasions, one is PC Rain and the other is PC Cold. The only downside of PC Rain is that he tends to cause an increase in Road Traffic Accidents (RTC), especially after a dry spell. Intertestingly RTCs use to be called RTA (Road Traffic Accident) until it was decided that the word accident meant that someone was liable. Anyway, the upside of PC Cold and PC Rain is that many of the naughty people seem to hate to either get wet or cold and crime often goes down on a wet night or during a cold spell. One cop I know with nearly 30 years service, has the thought that the recent drop in crime is due to less young white males being born a few years back, who statistically undertake most of the recorded crime. He feels that the recent baby boom will be felt in a few years with an increase in crime. An interesting theory, that only time will tell I suppose. Do people have less faith in the police than they use to, so report less? There are so many theories and suggestions for the peaks and troughs in crime figures. Personally I have seen crime rise and fall during my time, but I have never really been able to work out the why and how. As soon as I have a great theory, the naughty people go and disprove it!

As for the public I serve, I treat everyone with respect and try to be empathetic and understanding of their needs or issues. That approach has meant that I have yet to have a complaint made against me, even though I have undertaken some quite violent arrests. Everyone deserves to be treated with respect until provern otherwise. The greatest and most powerful piece of equipment a cop has is communication. The right approach and even tone can change an encounter or how people will react with you. I would much rather talk myself out of a situation than ending in a tustle or worse. Most will respond positively to the right approach; even admit what they have done on the odd occasion. All through, what in police speak is called tactical communication.

The key word is, 'listen' something the odd member of the public should learn when we try to explain or diffuse a situation. At times, maybe they are the ones that are in greater need of diversity training than the police. The public we serve do however sometimes leave us the funniest of telephone messages or even the odd email that can have you in stitches. I had this sent via a colleague, no idea if it is either true or real but made a grumpy old A Hole smile.

Dear Not so hot fuzz/automated telephone answering service

Having spent the past twenty minutes waiting for someone at Sandford police station to pick up a telephone I have decided to abandon the idea and try e-mailing you instead. Perhaps you would be so kind as to pass this message on to your colleagues in Sandford by means of smoke signal, carrier pigeon or Ouija board.

As I'm writing this email there are eleven failed medical experiments (I think you call them young people) in Camel Toe Street which is just off Relief Land Sandford. Six of them seem happy enough to play a game, which involves kicking a football against a garage door with the force of a meteorite. This causes an earth shattering CLANG! Which reverberates through my entire house. This game is now in its third week and as I am unsure how the scoring system works, I have no idea if it will end any time soon or if at all. The remaining five walking abortions are happily rummaging through several bags of rubbish and items of furniture that someone has so thoughtfully dumped beside the wheelie bins. One of them has found a saw and is setting about a discarded chair like a beaver on speed. I fear that it's only a matter of time before they turn their limited attention to the bottle of Calor gas that is lying on its side between the two bins. If they could be relied on to only blow their own arms and legs off or quietly kill themselves, I would happily leave them to it. I would even go so far as to lend them some form of fire manufacturing device. Unfortunately, they are far more likely to blow up half of Relief Land, along with themselves and I've only just finished decorating the lounge.

What I suggest to you is this, after replying to this e-mail with worthless assurances that the matter is being looked into and will be dealt with. Why not leave it until the one night of the year (probably bath night) when there are no mutants around then drive up the street in a police car before doing a three point turn and disappearing again. This will of course serve no other purpose than to remind us what policemen actually look like.

I trust that when I take a hammer to the skull of one of these throwbacks you'll do me the same courtesy of giving me a four month head start before coming to arrest me.

I remain sir, your obedient servant.

Judy Graham-Swallows

The beat manager for the area crafted a two-paragraph reply and received back the following reply:

Dear PC Rick O'Shea

First of all I would like to thank you for the speedy response to my original e-mail. 14 hours, 37 minutes and a few seconds, which must be a personal record for a Sandford Police station and be rest assured, that I will forward these details to the Guinness World Records for inclusion in their next book.

Secondly I was delighted to hear that our area has its own beat manager. May I be the first to congratulate you on your covert skills. In the five or so years I have lived on Relief Land, I have never seen you.

Do you hide up a tree or have you gone deep undercover and infiltrated the gang itself? Are you the one with the acne and the moustache on his forehead or the one with a chin like a wash hand basin? It's surely only a matter of time before you are headhunted by MI5 and in the running to be the new 007.

Whilst I realise that there may be far more serious crimes taking place in Sandford, such as smoking in a public place or walking without due care and attention. Is it too much to ask a police officer to explain, (using words of no more than two syllables at a time) to these twats, that they might want to play their strange football game elsewhere.
The pitch behind the Citadel or the one at JJB's are both within spitting distance, as is the bottom of the country park lake.
Should you wish to discuss these matters further you should feel free to contact me. If after 25 minutes I have still failed to answer, I'll buy you a large one in the Police Bar, where you all seem to spend more time than actually working.
I no longer remain sir, your obedient servant.
Judy Graham-Swallows

Enough of trying to make you feel guilty so you feel the need to make a donation to the police benevolent fund, and back to the story…

Sitting down in the car seat, I put the keys in the ignition. I reflected on another evenings work. It had not been a night any different to any other Friday night initially, with the usual jobs coming in - anti-social behaviour from bored youths and a suspicious vehicle. One youth, who requires special mention, is the one who thought it was a great idea to set alight a ping pong ball and throw it into a bin. That one ping pong ball caused one fire engine and two police cars to be dispatched at a cost of around £4000, and the loss of a poor defenceless yellow plastic bin. The youth was found hiding in a local toilet. We soon flushed him out and inconvenienced him with an £80 fine for criminal damage. As he wandered off with his £80 fine he shouted down the road back at me, "Yur mum so fat the police dogs stopped her at the airport for having 10 lbs of crack." That is another part of being a police officer - developing a thick skin to your many critics.

The only other slightly meatier job I had was a theft from the village supermarket. A cunning young man had walked in and filled up a basket with £87 worth of meat and three onions before he walked out and jumped into a waiting car. The haul consisted of one large Gammon joint, Brisket, Sirloin steaks and yes, three onions at a value of £1.50. A customer in the shop had witnessed the theft and reported it to a shop assistant. Sadly, the supermarket had failed to get details of the witness, so that was a line of enquiry closed to me. All I got was, "A young male went out with a basket full of meat and jumped into a blacked out car, with blacked out number plates." A quick look on the system for other incidents as I briefed myself on, stated that another male had struck 45 minutes earlier, in another village supermarket some six miles away. This seemed too much of a coincidence for it not to be a linked incident. The male that time had managed to get away with £150 worth of meat, although it had been put on the system wrongly and instead said £1500 worth of meat.

Enquiries on the great village meat theft are still ongoing. I will 'steak' my life on a lamb chop that the meat had been stolen to order…

It was, however, the call for a misdirected 999 call which would change the course of the evening, and turn it into fifty shades of poo. The initial call was reported to me as an abandoned 999 call, and sounded pretty much routine with nothing to worry about for a single crewed officer. I was just asked to go and check it out as a "concern for safety" for the female occupant who had rung in and then hung up.

It took quite a while to get there as the call was 10 miles from my location after dropping off a PCSO at another police station. I police a large rural area of larger and smaller sized villages on the fringe of a city that amounts to 135 square miles. My area extends to the borders of one of the two counties my force borders with. Sometimes it is just two cops covering that whole area, and never more than three, so to say I have the odd busy shift is an understatement. I have, on a couple of occasions, been the only available resource on a Saturday night, with 'jobs' (in police speak) stacking up such is the demand for my services.

The flat I was going to, was a notorious spot where a variety of social issues had manifested themselves. The flats themselves harboured people with mental health issue, drug users and some violent individuals. We regularly got calls about this block of flats, as more often than not, those problems would become our problems.

I finally located the flat after trying to work out how to get round the various barriers, that made it seem like Fort Knox to get in. On arrival, a member of the public came over to warn me about the flats being a "drugs den", almost as if I did not already know, or that I would be able to do something about it. Many of the residents living in the flats had friends in low places, the surrounding area being an ex-mining community. Some pockets of animosity towards the police still remained, long after the miner's strike in the 1980s. My Grandfather was a miner and the conditions they worked in, were far worse than anything I have had to put up with as a police officer. Many a Saturday night, was spent as a young lad at the miner's welfare, which is now a Tesco's.

I crossed over the road and walked up the badly paved path to the entrance, past some garages that were side-on to the flats. Only last year outside these same flats, the local ice cream man was found lying on the floor of his van covered in hundreds and thousands. I had to go and tell his wife, that he had topped himself.

I finally found and made my way in through the communal door, which was unusually unlocked. As I got up the first flight of stairs, covered in used cigarette butts, I was greeted by a female called Mildred, who lived in the flat. She must have seen me and rushed out of her flat to head me off. She approached me, eyes wide open in what seemed quite a flustered demeanour, "Sorry for calling you but I don't need the police now." I said that was fine but needed to make sure everything was ok, and I asked her if she was on her own, to which she said "no". I then said I would need to come in and check with them if everything was all right.

The flat was quite scruffy inside, with clothes strewn everywhere and toys and newspaper strewn all over the floor. Takeaway boxes flowed out of the kitchen bin and into the lounge, and a smell of stale curry lingered in the air. Seeing toys made me realise children were present, which only added to my concern. It was a situation that just did not feel right. There was also a male in the flat, called George, who was Mildred's boyfriend. They both admitted to a verbal altercation. Mildred said George had hurt her, George said, "No I haven't, you're just a fat cow."

George was quite thin and scruffy and had the look of someone who was a drug user. His eyes were wide and excitable, and even when talking quietly his demeanour went up and down quite rapidly. I knew at this point that I would have to deal with it as a domestic and do a full risk assessment.

The risk assessment was basically a checklist, which asked an assortment of questions that led to an overall score. This would then rate the person as a low, medium or high risk, in terms of further abuse or incidents of domestic abuse and how various agencies could offer support. Domestic abuse is no laughing matter and the police do take it seriously.

There had been previous incidents at the address, but I was unaware of any at that point. George was well known to the police; he had 20 odd pages of offences theft, robbery, and of course drugs, along with numerous arrests on his record. Oh, and did I mention that he also had anger management issues? It's a nice medical term for George being abusive and threatening.

George and Mildred thankfully agreed to my need to take further details and do a risk assessment. George just said, "Do what you have to do, but you need to remove my girlfriend's ex-partner Jeffery", who was the father of Mildred's children. George stated that Jeffery had an injunction and should not be here, something that Mildred backed up. Just talking about Jeffery got George agitated, and I said I would go and talk to him and ask him to leave.

Making my way outside, there were two males standing alongside a car, and in another car two children were sitting, who were Mildred's. The other male outside was her cross-dressing father, Ann, who Mildred had telephoned along with Jeffery, in what was becoming quite a bizarre situation. It was rapidly turning into a more and more complex situation. Jeffery was also quite agitated, making demands of what I should be doing as if he was some sort of armchair lawyer. At this point, my concern was focused on Mildred and her children, and I stated that Mildred had requested that he left the area as he was not local and must have travelled some fifteen miles to get there. Jeffery protested and demanded that I go inside and speak to her, which, after explaining the legal position, he still then ordered me to go and ask Mildred if she would speak to him, as he was understandably concerned for his children's safety.

I went back inside and explained what I had been told outside. This then caused George and Mildred to start arguing in very polite terms, as I stood in between them, as their very own referee. With George asking (in not very polite words) why Mildred had called Jeffery when he had allegedly raped her, she began to scream and shout at George as I tried to verbally calm the situation down. George decided he was going, "As it was, doin' his fucking head in". I followed him out and watched him get on his bike and ride past Jeffery. As he got to the end of the path he shouted back at the Jeffery, "I am gonna fucking kill you for raping my girlfriend." With this he turned left and rode off down the road away from the flat.

With George gone, I planned to go back inside and have a more in depth discussion about the whole situation, before starting the paperwork process and getting the risk assessment filled out. However, I still felt I was in a situation that was going to unravel, I was just not sure how and when. I had only been back in the flat a few seconds when Ann came rushing in, tripping over his heels for trying to walk far too quickly in a tight pencil skirt and saying, "You need to get outside quickly as they are fighting." I made my way outside to find both males bent over the bonnet of a car grappling with each other. George's bike and coat lay on the ground, and George and Jeffery were having a bit of a bun fight. This whole situation was like an episode of the Jerry Springer show and I was going to play the part of the bald headed bouncer breaking the fight up – even though I have a few more hairs on my head and am not even slightly as fearsome looking. As I made my way over to the fight, for only the second time in ten years I pressed the orange emergency button.

The emergency button basically gives you air priority and cuts off anyone else from speaking. It also raises the microphone sensitivity and there is no need to hit the talk button. I just asked for immediate assistance to my location as I had a fight in progress. Being at the location I was and knowing the locality of other units, I knew backup would take about 10 minutes, even with the other cops racing on blue lights to an assistance call. When a cop needs help you do tend to press on that little bit quicker, as it is a colleague in need of assistance and no one else is going to come to your aid.

I pulled Jeffery off first, and then grabbed George who had started the fight. I grabbed him by the shoulder and then carried out what is called a wrist lock. I then arrested him for assault, with Mildred protesting that I should not do so. George had yet again calmed down as I was arresting him, although was still shouting the odd profanity and, "I will kill you" comment at Jeffery.

The assault later turned into 'Common Assault and Threatening Words and Behaviour' when he was formally charged. George was still being abusive towards Jeffery as I handcuffed him. I moved George further away round the corner and he calmed down, before then becoming aggressive towards me, to the point where I got my CS spray out and threatened him with it by flipping the red cap up and pointing it towards him. I had no real intention of using it, as I was too close to spray without causing splash back on myself and the female. CS spray is nasty stuff and more often than not it is the police officers that have ended up with a bigger dose of the spray than the offender, either by being in the wrong place or the wind blowing the spray back at you.

At the distance I was from the George, I may have caused a serious eye injury to him which would have been disproportionate to the threat level I was encountering - which was basically just abusive and threatening words towards myself or anyone else that got close. A common belief is that police officers are allowed to use force, when in fact they can only use the force necessary for the incident or arrest. Any use of force has to be proportionate to the threat level, and always justifiable. Using CS spray at less than a metre and causing a serious or even minor eye injury would have been deemed as excessive use of force. I had full control and was only suffering verbal threats, although still in a threatening situation as a lone police officer. Excessive force is something you do have to consider when using any equipment or restraint technique. Even getting my CS spray out, without actually using it meant I needed to complete a use of force form stating the reasons for its withdrawal.

Finally, George calmed down, but then started to swear at a woman looking at what was happening. He did smell strongly of alcohol and I was not sure if he had taken anything else due to his very up and down demeanour.

After what felt like a very long 10 minutes, the cavalry arrived; first one car, then two, and finally three from another area. The various cops checked to see if I was ok and then started to get the various people inside so they could chat. I placed George into the back of a police car while I explained the situation to the other cops. Mildred told officers she was pregnant by George and Ann, Mildred's father told me she suffered from bi-polar disorder as I was taking details. After 10 minutes of action, it would now be time for several hours of paperwork. A domestic pack and risk assessment needed to be completed, and with witness statements gathered from all those involved, and I would need to do my arrest statement as well as convey George to the custody suite.

The police officers that turned up first took most of the initial workload. A special constable who was in his probation period needed to escort a prisoner with his tutor, as part of his tutor phase of training. Therefore, in the end, all I had to do personally that night was write a lengthy arrest statement. However, a large handover of paperwork awaited me the next day. This paperwork would form the file, which would be sent to the Crown Prosecution Service, as the arrest would most certainly end up in court. During checks on everyone involved, it turned out Jeffery did not have a full driving licence, and was not insured to drive the car he had driven to the flat in. As a result, he was arrested and charged by another colleague, for driving without insurance and driving otherwise than in accordance with a licence - a nice tick on his detections for the month, which at the time ran at three per month. A detection was basically being able to charge someone with an offence, and if you were running short for the month a drink driver was an easy target. Thankfully, that system has gone and was another great idea from the government in power at the time - to try and performance manage police officers.

Going to the dark side

So who in their right mind would want to be a police officer? Well, over 10,000 people apply each year, although that has dropped off since the recruitment freeze with only the odd forces currently recruiting. Of the 10,000 that apply, only 30% make it through the application stage and a further 40% through the SEARCH assessment centre. The assessment centre is where you get to play the role of a 'customer service advisor'. You get to deal with everything - from poorly performing staff, the Raggy Dolls who are out on day release from prison, to a customer who has complained about having criminals working with children. All the characters are played by actors who are either police staff or ex-police officers. The most important part is remembering to challenge any diversity issues, such as the man that says "Stupid blonde woman in her 4x4" or the woman who labels all criminals "idiots". More people fail on the diversity competencies than anything else. In fact, 70% of those that fail the assessment centre are due to a poor score on diversity, usually by missing or not challenging a diversity issue.

The variety of skills and backgrounds that police officers bring to many forces is quite vast. With many seeking career changes from being a teacher, solicitor or already in a Staff role within a police force. It is great to see the number of under represented groups now applying to become police officers; although more are still needed to be representative of the public the police serve.

Once you have made it into the police and through your first two years of probation, 'the job' does have good career progression and is a very varied job; at times even an exciting job, even though there are sometimes hours of being on a cordon or watching a prisoner, then the paperwork mountains to contend with. However, you do feel part of a team and the banter and camaraderie is something you will only ever experience in the police or the armed forces. If you look at police application forms, the most common reasons for joining are, "to serve the community" or "catch criminals." However, the real reason many apply is the perceived excitement that you do get, the thrill of a chase or responding to an incident with blue lights flashing. Some like the uniform and there are those outside of the uniform that have a thing for the handcuffs, but for the life of me I cannot see why as they are uncomfortable to wear. As a police officer you are never short of interesting stories to tell; some funny and some quite shocking. You do get to see a side of life that few others will ever see or even realise occurs just around the corner, or even next door to where they live.

People's views of the police are either that they sit around eating doughnuts at the police station all day, or what they have gleamed from the whole host of police TV shows. Some show the police in a good light, and some show us, as not being the brightest crayons in the packet, or worse, unpleasant, arrogant and would lie through our back teeth. It is fair to say that there are those that really should not be wearing a uniform and give the good ones a bad name. They have contempt for the public, and even each other at times; they tend to be the ones the public remembers, not the ones who try their best to help out and support others. A modern day police officer is a social worker, mediator, legal genius, problem solver and most of all, the one who people turn to in their hour of need. They deal with the worst that life has to throw at them day in and day out, and it is only fair to say that some come to distrust the human race. If for ten years you dealt with people who swore at you constantly, told lies and carried out a whole host of despicable acts on one another, would you be able to stay cool and collected day after day? You would have thought the police were there to investigate crime and catch criminals would you not? They indeed would, if it was not for the endless paperwork, which means at times they really do spend more time in the police station than patrolling the streets. Although technology is slowly changing that and ways of better deployment. However, when in the police station, an officer is unlikely to get injured, less being overzealous as they staple reams of paperwork together and staple their finger, or worse still suffer a life threatening paper cut. As funny as that statement is, each and every time a police officer steps out on the street, they are indeed putting themselves in harms way. There are those that have paid the ultimate price for simply do their job.

When someone rings in a report to the control room, rarely is anything as it seems, it is amazing how ten people become twenty and so on. A large fight is two youths having a slanging match. It is usually the ones that sound a bit too simple that often unravel into something much larger or unexpected. Often the person ringing 999 may have seen just one element of what has occurred or their perception of the incident. As a police officer, you have to investigate all elements if possible, whilst being impartial and not letting yourself prejudge, even though your instincts tell you otherwise.

I think the call handlers have a difficult job at times dealing with people phoning in to report a crime or incident. Sometimes these reports can be quite disturbing, and other times they can be quite funny.

A funny control room story, that I am really not sure is true or just urban myth, is about an individual, who had phoned in to report that thieves had been in their car. They said to the call handler, "Someone has broken into my car and they've stolen the dashboard, the steering wheel, the brake, the clutch - even the accelerator pedal!"

However, before an officer was sent, they rang again and said, "Never mind, I got in the back seat by mistake."

One of the most surprising elements I found other than some of the sights you see is the squalor some people live in. There are always the stories of the houses you visit, where you need to wipe your feet on the way out. I never realised people could live in such squalor and by choice, not through lack of money or ability. Just basic tidiness and hygiene really even with children running around dodging dog and cat mess, dead rodents and other such delights. Standards so low you did not dare to sit down or venture too far into the house. I have been in a house where you cannot see the floor for rubbish and the stench of human and animal excrement left in bags around the house filled the air.

However, nothing will ever compare to the very sad smell of a body that has been left for a week or two to decompose inside. Sadly, the winter brings sudden deaths and often these elderly people go unnoticed for weeks before someone phones in concerned. The police get the job of entering by force usually with a strong inkling of what we are about to find. The sad fact is that some elderly people do get forgotten as families move away or the community around them changes.

Other stories of the strange things people get up or do, such as the thief who in custody shoved an earring up his bottom. The doctor was the funniest part of that story as she told him he was just "full of shit" literally his bowels on the X-ray were rather full. Although, I was not sure if she was just being sarcastic to the male. There are the criminal's that have graduated from the school of stupidity whom think that they will never get caught. Even though they have had a drink of milk in the house they have just burgled, and left the dirty cup along with some nice DNA. Then there are those that commit offences in clear view of CCTV so you get their full face or boast about their haul on Facebook.

As for the police officers who join, there is still the element of police officers who joins to be the 'big man'. They like the feeling of power wearing a police uniform gives. I have always felt more of a target not less of a target when out in uniform.

It is true to an extent that some cops were once bullied and can now boss other people around. Sometimes being a bit too heavy handed or maybe the excessive use of force. I will say those types are getting less and less as professional standards are very hot on anything that could cause the force to be brought into disrepute, or standards that fall below what is expected of a police officer. Cops that sail a bit too close to the wind or cut too many corners are ones that other cops class as "dangerous" and other cops, will avoid working with. The worst type of cops, are those that seem so amiable and polite yet would sell their own mother in order to get themselves out of a tight spot. Usually these are the types, which have no integrity either. Their ego is huge, unable to take any form of criticism and think they know it all. These are also dangerous to work with, not because they will get you killed but they will get you in a situation, that could well come back and bite you in the bottom years down the line. Police like any job be it a teacher or an office worker, has those that do both a good and a bad job. The greater number are the ones that are highly professional and go beyond the call of duty to support a victim or ensure an investigation is thoroughly carried out.

These days you have to follow policies and procedures to protect yourself from internal as well as external trouble. Social media is one example where it is all too easy to post something in jest that then causes offence and professional standards get involved and end up being disciplined. Understandably, you are a police officer and as such, a person of standing so high expectations of conduct and integrity are to be expected. However, by following procedures and advice it keeps you on the right side of the law and your job. I have seen five special constables sacked in the last year, along with two regular cops that were sacked and a further two that resigned before they were sacked. So with all this, why after nearly ten years am I still a police officer?

Initially I must admit it was for the action and the thrill of a chase, the adrenaline rush responding to an emergency is quite a buzz. Chasing after someone running away and catching them is another pure adrenaline rush. Being in a police car that is travelling at speed with blue lights is very exciting the first few times after that for me anyway. These days I can feel a bit queasy travelling at speed along winding country lanes, especially with a very fast driver and all four wheels leave the road over a humped back bridge.

Being able to make a difference is the part that has never changed, knowing you have done the right thing. Maybe helped to give someone a positive experience of the police or been there in their time of need. The police like many industries are more and more customer focused with a great emphasis on managing expectations so our customers have a realistic expectation of what we can and will do.

As the years have progressed, it is not really just the action that draws me to continue, but the camaraderie. I enjoy the banter and working as part of a team. I get to do something very different to the '9-5er's'and have never stopped learning from the day I joined. On the odd occasion, I have made a difference, trying not to sound too arrogant even saved lives and property.

Then of course, cops can do and say the most hilarious things. Such as the classic story, I heard about a traffic police officer who had stopped a female driver for speeding. He walked over to the car and asked the female driver to get out. The female driver got out of the car and said, "I guess you want to sell me some tickets to the Policeman's Ball?" The police officer slightly taken aback responded, "Police Officers don't have balls, Miss." The Police officer realising what he had just said, decided the best course of action was a, "Umm well don't let me catch you speeding again". He then quickly got in his car and drove off.

Training

On a bright April morning, I made my way to training school. I had just moved house the day before as mad as that sounds. My training dates came through, as is often the case in life, everything happens at once, as the day after I got my police training dates I sold my house. Therefore, even though the house was still in a mess and I had spent the night sleeping on the floor. It may amaze you to know that police officers are now quite highly trained and mandatory courses from Child Protection, Diversity, to MOPi (Management Of Police information) are thrust upon us via eLearning portals. I know some police officers make Forest Gump look like Steven Hawkins - OK only joking. The number with degrees ranging from maritime studies to fashion unrelated to the police shows the diverse cross section of people who want to become police officers. The role does demand a certain level of intellect, at times way above my own intellect I feel at times. Confidence is a key element -

something I did not initially possess and during training I got told it was something I needed to build on. The next day I came back to training with a Lego model, the rest of the cohort thought it was hilarious, as for the Lego model well it was just a Lego police car complete with working flashing lights!

My initial training consisted of 12 weeks of training school, and 10 weeks working on the streets with a tutor. This was the first week of 12 that would take me from civilian to fully-fledged police officer. 12 weeks or 60 days, to learn all about law, role of a police officer, dealing with different incidents, basic army drill and using all the lovely equipment that if I am honest has, as many up's as down's in actual use. The lovely equipment included an extendable baton or ASP, which will only survive a few hits before it collapses. CS spray that ends up either blowing back on to yourself or fellow cops making your own eyes water so you cannot see. Worse still you spray a person who is immune to the CS spray, dogs are also immune to CS spray. Much to everyone's surprise CS is actually a crystal not a gas. It is theses CS crystals that cause irritation in your pores or tear ducts. For police use it is dissolved in industrial paint stripper used to clean ships and it is that which causes all the redness around the eyes. The solvent is designed to dissolve body fat and open pores to enable the CS crystals to reach the tear ducts and cause irritation. My brain hurt at the thought of what I was about to undertake and what the training would entail. In fact one person decided after three days it was all too much for them and quit. I bumped into them a year later and they were an area manager for Burger King. So I got a Whopper on the house, as in burger, before any rude thoughts cross your mind. The best part about training was bonding as a cohort, mine was cohort 13 and you really do make some lifelong friends as you support each other through the highs and the lows of training. After three day's of law your head would be pounding, even the IT training was challenging such as learning to use the Police National Computer (PNC) desktop system. With 36 different fields that can be used to search and outputting all manner of information that needed to be interpreted. The search is based on what is known as the Soundex system. Developed by Robert C. Russell and Margaret K. Odell in 1918 and used initially in the New York docks to index names by sound, to aid with the vast number of migrant workers.

Our training consisted of the first week being designed to introduce us to our force and gain an understanding of policing. It was designed to give us a good grasp of how the force works and what they were trying to achieve. Including the latest strapline, that was drilled into us so we could reel it off. We looked at our forces aims and policing style, along with how they provide a service that meets the needs of everyone in the community. We also looked at how being a police officer affects your life, also what being a police officer meant to you and your family. We got given the opportunity to discuss with the rest of the intake our hopes and fears about becoming a police officer. On one of the sessions the Chief Constable came to visit us, he spoke of how being a police officer can mean you end up in situations that may be quite difficult to handle. The Chief Constable then turned to the student officer next to me and said, "What would you do if you had to arrest your mother?" To which the student officer replied, "Call for backup!" That was it, everyone was howling with laughter including the Chief Inspector. That same officer is now an Inspector and still telling howlers every once in a while.

In the end, being a police officer is a job that for some strange reason the people we lock up do not tend to like us very much. Even though, when in custody they get a few cups of hot tea and a microwave meal on the house.

At various stgaes of training we had a bit of IT training, this has now become quite a large part of the course for current recruits. Some of which they even do online via the National Centre for Applied Learning Technologies (NCALT) system. Where you read and click away, do a knowledge check and have a lovely little certificate generated for you bedroom wall. New recruits now have to learn how to use the Force intranet as part opf a one day course then Human resource systems, intelligence systems, business and crime systems and the Police

National Computer (PNC). In total they have 39 Business applications and 31 intelligence applications to learn. Some you may only use once a year depending on your job role and the sorts of crimes and jobs you have dealt with.

On the third and fourth weeks we had our Officer Safety Training (OST), which is designed to give us the skills we will need to deal with situations on the street. The fifth and sixth weeks looked at radio usage, IT systems and equality and diversity. The police radios are worthy of a mention as they are just as good as they are bad. They have GPS so you can always be located, great for a safety point, but not so great for those officers that liked to sneak home off area for their tea. It also means control knows that you are just around the corner from a job no one wants to attend, the excuse "Is anyone closer" is very hard to use.

The radios are in essence mobile phones, which you can use as a telephone as well as sending text messages. By keying in the collar number of a police officer; you can also do what is called a point to point. This is basically, just using it as a radio between two people. Like all technology, it is not without its problems. Signal loss especially in the rural area, I police is a problem. One night, it was so bad I ended up using my own mobile phone. Clear cold nights can be the worst, when it sounds like you are talking from inside a biscuit tin, and end up shouting into the radio to be heard. We all know what it is like to lose the signal on your mobile phone well police radios are just the same, although our radios give quite a disconcerting beep, beep to let you know you're screwed if you need to use the radio. The same can be said of the Blackberry's we all now carry to enable us to access mobile data. A great piece of kit and highly useful – even if the public think we are texting a mate whilst standing talking to them. When in reality we are making notes or putting data in to undertake a PNC search. Being a mobile phone and using mobile phone data, they too like everyday mobile phones suffer from the same good and bad signal areas.

During training we had two trainers who sat in two chairs on opposite sides of the room. When one stood up the other sat down in the most bizarre manner. After the initial ice breaker that I always loath and hate - due to having to say other silly things about myself or play some silly game to let people know more about myself. We got down to the first task of writing on a flip chart in groups what we thought the role of a police officer was and its effects on our lives and family.

A very interesting place to start I thought, the variety of answers were just as interesting. Everything from being a good cop to catch robbers and murderers went up on the various pieces of paper. I could not help drawing some silly mister men pictures on our group's flip chart paper, just to add some interest. The whole morning was pretty much an introduction to what being a police officer was all about. The weeks training did actually go quicker than expected. By Friday afternoon my head was spinning like mad, with the amount of material we had digested. We all got issued with a variety of books for a nice bedroom read or simply a cure for insomnia. I was no better in training than at school, never doing my homework or just doing it at the last minute by finding the course 'swot' and copying theirs.

The second week we looked at the various forms that we might need to fill out. The amount of paperwork came as quite a shock and made me wonder how a police officer actually manages to get out of the police station and on patrol. To be honest, there are times when you don't make it out of the station for a whole shift whilst you take a few layers off your paperwork mountain, under the watchful eye of a sergeant. Often there is duplicate or even triplicate information that needs recording, which has always seemed barmy to me. They say the law is an ass, maybe it is not the law, but the amount of paperwork it attracts is the ass side of things? We have packs for burglary, robbery and domestic violence and all have different forms to fill in.

As a rough guess, we have about 30 mainstream forms then a whole plethora of other forms stored electronically for recording this and that. Sometimes you can spend four to six hours just sorting out the paperwork for a full file. A full file is all the information needed by the CPS in order to prosecute. Although you can do all that work and the CPS decide there is insufficient evidence or no case to answer and the case is dropped. Which can be very frustrating for the cops who have done all the leg work investigating the crime and filling in reams of paperwork!

Court makes for an interesting insight into a world that seems years behind. By that, I mean the reams of paper everyone carries and the reliance on bits of paper. If one bit of paper is lost then a whole case can be thrown out, or if one piece of paper has been filled in incorrectly again the case can be thrown out of court. In court as a police officer, you do get cross examined and probed. Once I was asked as a first question from the defence, "So officer, how far is it from the police station to the crime scene?" I said I don't know as I had not travelled from the police station but was about six miles. They then said, "So you are just guessing how far it is then? So there is no point asking how far it would be to the crime scene from Barnsley then?" All I could reply to that was, "I would either use a Sat Nav, or look it up on

Google maps." I did get a wry smile out of the magistrate for that reply, the solicitor just said, "There will be no need for that officer."

My all-time favourite story that a colleague told me was, when the defence was cross-examining a police officer during a trial at crown court.

"*Officer, did you see my client fleeing the scene?*"

"*No sir, but I subsequently observed a person matching the description of the offender running across the local park.*"

"*Officer, who provided this description?*"

"*The officer who was first on the scene, and past on the initial description from a witness.*"

"*So you are saying a fellow officer provided the description of this so-called offender. Do you trust your fellow officers?*"

"*Yes, with my life.*"

"*With your life indeed? Let me ask you this then officer, do you have a locker room in the police station, a room where you change your clothes in preparation for your daily duties?*"

"Yes, we do."

"And do you have a locker in that room?"

"Yes, I do."

"And do you have a lock on your locker?"

"Yes, I do."

"Now why is it, officer, if you trust your fellow officers with your life, but you find it necessary to lock your locker in a room you share with those officers?"

"You see sir, we share our building with the magistrates court, and sometimes defence solicitors have been known to walk through that room."

The theory training continued in earnest, would you believe we could spend a whole week on form filling? Well, nor did I until I endured it for myself and sent my head spinning once more. After two weeks, I was really beginning to question my rationale for joining up, as so far all I got was a headache. If this was the training what would it be like being on the street? It certainly seemed less and less like the soap opera "The Bill" or any other of the numerous television programs showing all the exciting bits of being a cop but very little of the form filling or hours on the phone trying to get through to CPS direct.

I have to admit the law week returned my faith in what I was doing. We covered all the basic and some more complex offences such as theft, assault, robbery and burglary. It all seemed pretty simple and straightforward on paper. If they had committed this then they had broken that law and could be charged with this and so on. Anyone could do this police bit, why was I worrying it was all so easy! The definitions and how to apply the law was the hard bit and that would come later….

Take burglary as an example by definition it was just Burglary is defined by section 9 of the Theft act 1968, which created two variants:

"A person is guilty of burglary if he enters any building or part of a building as a trespasser with intent to steal, inflict grievous bodily harm (or raping any person therein), or do unlawful damage to the building or anything in it. (Section 9 (1) (a))"

"A person is guilty of burglary if, having entered a building or part of a building as a trespasser, he steals

or attempts to steal anything in the building, or inflicts or attempts to inflict grievous bodily harm on any person in the building (section 9(1)(b))"

For the crime to be complete certain elements outlined below need to be met.

Enters - although physical evidence of entry is not normally difficult to obtain, it can be difficult on occasions to decide whether an entry has occurred in law.

Building or part of a building - the Theft act 1968 does not define a building, so this must be a matter of fact for the jury, however, section 9 (3) specifically states that the term includes an "inhabited vehicle or vessel"; hence motor homes, caravans and houseboats are protected by the section even when temporarily unoccupied. Burglary can also be committed in "part of a building" and in R v Walkington 1979 the defendant had entered a large shop during trading hours but went behind a counter and stole money from the till. The court held that he had entered that part of *the building normally reserved for staff as a trespasser and was therefore guilty of burglary.*

As a trespasser - the essence of trespass is entering or remaining on another's property without authority; a person having permission to enter property for one purpose who in fact enters for another purpose may become a trespasser: an example being, a friend invited you into their property and you then stole some jewellery. In recent years, the terms "distraction burglary", "artifice burglary" and "burglary by trick" have been used in crime prevention circles when access to premises is granted as a result of some deception on the occupier, usually by pretence that the burglar represents somebody who might reasonably request access such as a water, gas or electricity supplier. There is no separate legal definition of this variant.

With intent - the intention to commit an offence, being an essential element of burglary, requires proof beyond reasonable doubt. For example, if entry is made to regain property which the defendant honestly believes he has a right to take, there is no intention to steal and the defendant is entitled to be acquitted. However, it has been held that a conditional intent to steal anything found to be of value is enough to satisfy this requirement.

I must mention Human Rights, which is still a contentious issue in many circles. Some good cops left with the implementation and in practice are a mixed blessing. I have always believed anyone who has committed a criminal offence has in some way negated some of their human rights. But at present that is not seen as the case. We have had the so called "Bill of Rights" banded about as a replacement or partial substitution. At present many people believe that Human Rights seems to be used more as a "get out of jail card" and the common complaint with the British public is the offenders have more rights than the victims.

The Human Rights Act 1998 gives further legal effect in the UK to the fundamental rights and freedoms contained in the ECHR. These rights not only impact matters of life and death, they also affect the rights you have in your everyday life: what you can say and do, your beliefs, your right to a fair trial and other similar basic entitlements.

Most rights have limits to ensure that they do not unfairly damage other people's rights. However, certain rights – such as the right not to be tortured – can never be limited by a court or anybody else.

An example of human rights in practice is that you cannot parade a shop thief through the store and you should try to hide the handcuffs if you cannot leave by a rear entrance. In our current litigation culture it is essential that you understand human rights and the treatment of anyone in your care or are dealing with. As of yet touch wood (place hands on my head) I have yet to have a complaint made against me. Maybe I have been lucky or maybe I have not given cause for complaint. I believe in being fair but firm, I treat people in the same manner I would want to be treated. Other than the odd person who is anti-police or believe they are being victimised by the police. Most people respond quite well to a polite and courteous approach, even if they have committed a criminal offence.

With week three completed, I had the pleasure of going to HQ during the week to pick up all my uniform and kit. It was quite a weighty load to carry. The batons alone that the Police wield look so light and flimsy at the TV but in reality must be 800g+ in weight. The handcuffs were defiantly not built for comfort and more on that later. Along with handcuffs and a baton I got issued two white shirts, a black clip on tie, police fleece, high visibility police jacket, jumper, two pairs of trousers, the traditional British police custodian helmet, utility belt, limb restraints. The actual boots were down to me to buy.

The kit we carry does add up to a fair bit of weight and I have lost my balance and fallen over a couple of times due to the extra weight of my kit, much to the amusement of my fellow cops. The stab vest seems to alter your centre of gravity and you end up a bit like a Weeble. One night on foot patrol just before Christmas, I managed to walk to close to the edge of the curb and in trying to catch my balance, I fell over. Right in front of a large group of males, who was crying with laughter at such a sight. I quickly got back up and said, "I have only had one can of coke"

I then spent four days learning how to use CS Spray, handcuffs, Asp, and limb restraints. The first of the two more hands on weekends look at Unarmed Defence Tactics. This was supposed to be how we protected ourselves from the naughty person, who decided maybe I was not being quite as nice and friendly as I should be. It was supposed to be a mixture of Jujitsu and Judo and came together to form what looked more like a form of oriental ballet dancing, whilst shouting the words "BACK OFF, BACK OFF". Personally if a big bad man was coming towards me and I was on my own, I would most likely just run like hell and probably achieve the four minute mile in the process. Better to retreat and live to see another day, than try to be a hero. A really violent offender can take four of five cops to control safely and without injury.

The second weekend we got to try out our extendable batons or ASP's and learn various techniques for hitting people including the areas we could and could not hit unless in mortal danger. The so called, "red areas" which was the head, neck, torso and groin. This was followed by using the CS spray, we all got to take a whiff of the nasty stuff and it truly made your eyes water. A popular misconception of CS is that it is a gas. When in actual fact that is just a delivery method. As I said earlier CS is actually a small crystal and it is that, that causes all the irritation. Dogs and some humans are immune to it though.

After having sampled, smelling the stuff and rather than everyone ending up in hospital actually using live CS. We were trained to; 'shoot' the CS using canisters filled with water. This ended up more as a water fight than anything else. The final part of the weekend was using the handcuffs. Who would have thought you had so many different ways to handcuff a naughty person. Front, rear, stack the mind boggled. This was when I really did learn these handcuffs were nothing like the pink fluffy ones from Ann Summers. Not that I have tried them I would like to add, before you all start to get strange idea's about cops with pink fluffy handcuffs.

All I can say after being handcuffed at least 10 times, my wrists were red raw and rather sore. It looked like I had been self-harming such were the marks and subsequent bruises on my wrists. Now I felt sorry for the naughty person I would have to at some point use these on. For now, I would let my wrists recover before preparing for my first shift on duty. I do recommend the pink fluffy ones from Ann Summers, as they are actually quite comfy. This was the final week before we spent 40 hours on duty before returning for a final two weeks of training. Now I would get to put all that training into practice. I intended to arrest at least three people and solve at least one crime by the end of my first shift. After all how hard could being a cop be?

First Shift

I arrived half an hour before my shift was due to start at 4pm. I had had a tour of the station the previous week so knew where all my locker and changing room were. The fun part was getting ready, as nobody had told me how I should actually wear my uniform as silly as that sounds. I tried to put on my epaulettes and they ended up looking more like floppy dog's ear's, all because I forgot to attach them to a button on my shirt. The stab vest took a bit of playing with to get it on and fitted right. The rest of the kit was not too bad, although my kit belt seemed to have a mind of its own and I ended up putting it on upside down, which looking back now was quite an amazing feat!

Finally suited and booted, I made my way to the parade room feeling as if I was on my first day at school and too shy to speak to anyone. I shuffled into the parade room trying not to be noticed and stood in a corner out of the way. I had phoned the police officer who was due to be my tutor the previous week. She taught me well and many things she taught me have stuck with me. She has to be one of the best and most knowledgeable cops I have ever worked with. Also very outspoken and I would imagine possibly one reason she has not made it to sergeant yet; along with the fact like many cops prefers to be on the beat instead of behind a desk. Thankfully after a few minutes of loitering in the parade room, she came through the door and sorted me out and got me dressed properly before the briefing started.

    As soon as I sat down various cops sized me up without really saying anything. You do have to prove yourself and everyone is waiting to see how you shape up in a difficult situation and will you get stuck in. Some of the cops I have worked with over the years have been quite interesting. I have worked with PC Angry who seemed to always be angry with someone he would even be angry even at the nicest person. The way he spoke to people was truly awful at times. Another regular cop does not like altercations and they will actively keep away from fights or violent crimes if they can. The same can be said of some specials. One special actually asked me how to wind the windows down in a police van; this was the same special that had to get off duty at 9pm so he could get to bed by 10pm. This was not because of work or children just because he liked getting up early in the morning to watch television. As you may imagine they only lasted about 6 months after letting a prisoner run off into the night complete with handcuffs. A special constable who is not very good at being a cop is referred to as a, 'uniform carrier'. Let's not forget though, that these individuals are giving up their spare time unpaid to serve their local community, with many wanting to become full-time officers.

Anyway, back to my first shift. My first shock was how few police officers there were in the area that we covered. Three cops and a sergeant not including myself was the thin blue line for an area of over 20 square miles. Since then it has dropped to two or three across most of my force with the government cops and experienced cops being asked to retire. Then cheekily sent a letter asking them if they would like to become Specials Constables and volunteer for the job they just got pushed out of.

Briefing began, with the sergeant going through everything that had happened and local intelligence and what to look out for, pretty basic stuff and I scribbled reams of notes into my pocket notebook thinking I was dead clever. As the other cops just sat and listened. I was going to catch that car thief red handed and that prolific burglar he would be dead easy to catch in the act. How would we cope with all the naughty people stealing and generally being badly behaved?

With briefing over and a few grunts of hello from the other regular officers on the shift, I set off out with my tutor for the first time. We climbed into a one year old police car that already had over 1000,000 miles on the clock and the seats had been torn by handcuffs and was filled with the smell of stale beer and chips. Quite a few of the Police cars have had new engines over the years. One poor Volvo T5 was driven through a very large puddle and water got into the engine, causing £7000 of damage. I have only seen one police car written off in a head on collision and another severely damaged, as it was rammed by a 4x4 trying to get away. To be fair considering the abuse the cars get, they are very reliable but I would never touch an ex-police car having seen the hard life they lead.

Out on the open road my tutor began to ask me about my full time occupation prior to joining, and why had joined. The very same questions I had been asked during training. After about half an hour on patrol, we got our first call to a small fire on a local playground caused by local youths. The fire brigade was on scene but wanted us to attend, both for protection and investigation. Sadly, it is all too common for the local youths to be abusive to the fire brigade or thrown stones at a distance. Strangely, I have yet to be called to aid paramedics because of the 'hoodie brigade'; it is usually the person they are treating that is being difficult. I have made my own hospital run on occasions; mainly to drop off patients with mental health issues that have been left to live on their own, when really they should be being looked after in a shelter or warden aided accommodation.

We made our way on blue lights to the park and the thrill of driving above the speed limit with the blue lights flashing really got the adrenaline pumping. There was also the thrill of the unknown, wondering what I would find as we raced to the scene. On arrival there was a small group of youths hanging around watching the fire brigaded at work. Someone had set fire to a bin on the playground and being plastic had simply melted on to the ground below it.

Not one of the little darlings we spoke to knew anything, or more than likely did not want to say anything. So that was my first unsolved crime, no arrest and no naughty person detained. It would be recorded as an undetected criminal damage. So maybe I was not quite the Sherlock Holmes I thought I would be. After that we went back on patrol and spent another hour driving round in circles seeing if we could find anything to do. The radio was all quiet on our side, the other area that we shared our talk group with seemed allot more lively with cops being sent to thefts and domestics. I yearned for some more action, rather than driving round in circles, when a call for a fight in a local pub came in. Again the blue lights went on and we sped the short drive to the scene. Expecting to get hands on and be pulling people off one another, I made myself mentally ready. On arrival at the pub, everything was quiet and nothing to see. We got out and went into the pub and again nothing? Was this a hoax call? My tutor spoke to the landlord and he said it had just been a couple of guy's pushing and shoving each other and had then left.

This was my first lesson in the fact that when Joe public phoned the police it was more often than not quite as bad as reported. 50 youths would be 15; a group fighting could be friendly jostling between them. A serious car crash could just be a minor fender bender. Now with a few years' service the adrenaline no longer pumps and I always go with an open mind taking on board the details but not making any judgments until I have arrived and I am dealing with the incident. Even with blue lights whaling it fails to stir me, the only thing that does stir me is car sickness with some police drivers, they are excellent drivers and very quick, just as a passenger I start to feel a bit queasy. In some ways, it is like being a fire fighter who is scared of heights, over a certain height.

We jumped back into the police car and did a short search for the men involved in the altercation, but as expected no trace. Yet another unsolved crime. I began to wonder what the police actually did, at the moment we just seemed to react and then if we were lucky maybe catching someone.

That was the end of the action for the rest of the shift. My tutor had some CCTV to pick up from a petrol station that had suffered a 'bilkin' the word used to denote driving off with fuel without paying for it. The 8 hours on duty seemed to have just flown by even though we had maybe 30 minutes of action followed by 7 and a half hours of nothing. I could not wait to get back on duty the following Friday, seven days almost seemed too long. After a quick debrief with my tutor I made sure I filled out my pocket notebook, as it had been drilled into us during training the importance of keeping it up to date and was a legal document.

My head pounded from information overload, I realised that being a police officer was a very big job indeed. The amount of knowledge required to be competent seemed vast. Dealing with people had been a little nerve wracking as had my attempts to use the radio, getting tongue tied and saying the wrong thing. The worse thing about the radio was that everyone else on the same channel could hear what you were saying as well.

My tutor did a good job of calming me down, as she could see I looked a little panic stricken. She told me not to worry and just take my time. These very same words I have used with all the student officers I have taken out since becoming a tutor constable myself.

Being a cop seems so easy on TV, but the cameras fail to show the paperwork and procedures that have to be followed. The statements that need to be written, and can take up to a couple of hours to write. In fact, statements are such a major part of police work. For more low-level crimes such as theft, minor assault, harassment we have a special car that goes out to take them. One force has labelled one police car as the, "Facebook" car as it deals with quite a few incidents related to Facebook. Mainly when someone has told them they are a female dog, put a rather bad picture up, whispered a sweet nothings on their wall, which are not quite so sweet and so on. Why people do not just block or contact Facebook in the first place before contacting the police I will never know... social networking is consuming more and more police time. The more communication mediums people have the more mediums they have to be malicious to one another.

In 2008, there were just 556 reports of 'social network' crimes; last year there were 4,908 a rise of 800%. In 2011, 653 people were charged for crimes involving Facebook and Twitter.

Never Volunteer

My Inspector had sent an email asking for volunteers for a summer fate on our division. Being the new green and keen cop, I madly volunteered to do both days on over-time, without realising fully what it would entail. Would I do the same now, I think the words Foxtrot Oscar spring to mind and I will let you deduce what it means. I am more than happy to do anything for my rota be it to step in whilst they attend a school play their child is in, or need to leave early for one reason or another. However, give up two day's to help another area out, is now a no no, partly as I now have a family but also soon realised that you don't actually get much thanks for what you do. More often than not just getting used and abused. The overtime is nice but there has to be the correct work/life balance, some cops seem to do endless amounts of overtime. Personally, I would rather spend time with Mrs Hole and the little Hole's. Although Mrs Hole at times I am sure would rather I was at work. Anyway, I turned up at the police station at 8am in the morning and awaited my transport to the fair. We had been pretty much tasked with spending the whole day directing traffic at various locations and helping the stewards in the very large field that was to be a car park. So I spent 8 hours standing on the side of the road stopping traffic and directing traffic into a car park. My feet ached and throbbed although I did get relived for half an hour to go and eat my police supplied packed lunch. Several special constables were also helping out, who in their right minds would volunteer to stand on a roadside for eight hours? I take my hat off to special constables giving up their free time to help their local force, and at times is a thankless task.

   Sunday was much of the same, although I was let off my leash a little and allowed to do some foot patrol around the fair itself. This was when I made the first mistake of my career as a special. Walking round the fair we had reports of loud bangs from one corner of the fate and I made my way over there with several other officers en-route. On arrival, I spoke to a man about the bangs and got onto the radio feeling very proud to announce it was a, "Firearms" incident. Well this caused all sorts of things to take place, armed response were mobilised all the other cops were put on a high state of alert and a sergeant would come and join me to get further details. Behind one of the stalls, there was a lad with some fireworks and the other one was carrying a battery. When the other cops arrived, one of the lads was charged and the other was let off.

As the bangs were simply fireworks thrown by local kids, the sergeant quickly got on the radio to announce it was not a firearms incident, before armed response arrived. He looked at me and shook his head in a slightly frustrated manner; I thought it best to go back to directing traffic, where I could cause the least damage possible. It is amazing how quickly you learn from your mistakes and that would be the first of a few during my early career as a cop.

Two day's on my boots had not been kind to my long suffering feet and had a few blisters in which to hobble around work come Monday morning. I had done a seven-day week and had another day off before back to another stretch of six days on duty.

I have learnt not to volunteer unless I know exactly what I will be doing. Like many institutions, communication is nearly non-existent, at times the arse and the elbow have no idea what each was doing. The greatest plans would fall apart due to minor details being missed out. Such as lack of transport to get there or the person leading the operation being off sick, and not telling anyone what they had planned.

I have done some very enjoyable and pleasant operations over the years though. From marathons to bike rides, what makes it enjoyable is the atmosphere and the ability to interact with the public, showing police officers in a good light. I met my wife on one such operation although it was a chance meeting on duty that led to another chance meeting off duty and then the fairy tale story unfolded, well the fairy tale bit is a lie but don't tell my wife. However, I am still happily married after six years, even though at times I am sure she would be very happy if I quit being a cop and spent more time at home and not work quite so many unsociable hours.

Back at training school for the final two weeks, everyone was full of interesting 'war stories' of what they had done during their initial tutoring of duty. One person had made three arrests to my zero. Wanting to be a super cop was much harder than I initially thought. The training we would get this week was on using our radio's, which was a great idea after we had already spent a fair few hours trying to get to grips with them. We also went through the various IT systems and programs that we could use to aid us. Some systems had a specific way to input information especially the, "Crimint" system that used to be mentioned at least twice an episode on the TV show, 'The Bill'. This intelligence application had a set way you had to input the data otherwise; the search function would not work. To this day, I still have to refer to my crib sheet to remember if I am inputting details in the correct format.

The final weeks training was equality and diversity training - we all were put on a bus to take us to a community centre. This was to have chat, to some young people from a variety of cultures and backgrounds.

These young people were the ones that were happy to talk to the police and not the more usual surely or evasive young people you met on the street. I have to admit I found it an interesting and in some ways eye opening situation. Since the Steven Laurence murder, the police as a whole have become more focused on equality, diversity, and stamp out institutional racism, which I must admit I have never seen or come across personally. The number of ethnic officers is still quite low and there are still at least 2-3 male cops for every female cop. As I said, some of the tolerance is closer to home with some full-time cops unwilling to accept either special constables or PCSO's. When I joined, specials were told they could not go out with a PCSO on health and safety grounds. To me it always seemed more of a political rule, which became null and void with Specials being aligned to work with the newly created Neighbourhood Police Team's or NPT for short. We lost the really good special that use to regularly come out with the shift to NPT. Thankfully, since the cuts and drop in numbers, specials have been allowed to come back and work with response. We are grateful for the extra pair of hands, providing they are not a liability and we don't have to explain each and everything ten times over. All we want is a special who will back us up and get stuck in when the chips are down.

I must mention PCSO's as they do sometimes get undeserved bad press. Even though they do not have the same powers as police officers, they still carry a lot of responsibility, and have over time become a crucial part of the police force I work for. Along with special constables, they have been established to work with their partners to ensure the right people, the right numbers and with the right skills, are in the right place at the right time although the last part is not quite true and I will cover that later. The PCSO's I have worked with have been a great source of intelligence and up to date knowledge of the area. Especially when as a cop you cover a much wider area, and do not always know all the local criminals quite as well.

With the two final weeks complete that was it, looking back the training we received was actually very good and I did enjoy it. Even though really we only scratched the surface of law, never mind all the various form filling and procedures you had to follow. I was now on probation for two years and would continue to work with my tutor for another six months before being allowed to go solo.

Many cops will tell you how much they enjoyed training even if we were all chomping at the bit dying to get out on the streets. Out of the fifteen that started my course, eleven are still cops. Three of my intake were lost in the first year and the other one resigned and went to be an airport firefighter a few years back.

Back on the Front Line

As a keen and very green cop, I was eager to learn more and strove to be as good as any other cop. My keenness did get me into trouble, as I would react without thinking or the old adage, "fools rush in" was quite applicable to the way I was during my first six months. I have never dared ask how much of a pain I was to some of my fellow cops I worked with during my first few months of duty. I must have got on some of their nerves with my keenness to get out of the station or try to get stuck in or make wrong judgments. Once I read my A to Z wrong and sent the cop I was with to the right street name, just on the wrong side of the city. The joys of being young in service… thankfully it has been largely forgotten, but as with anything you have to start somewhere and learn from your mistakes to move forward and improve. Some of the best cops I know have made some corking cock ups from the car's in ditches to missing people hiding in the loft. A new cop does look new and often will lack confidence or be in a bright and shiny new uniform, and if any of them are like me as a student officer, I would advise to stay clear!

I still remember my first arrest It is strange how clear it still is, almost like the veritable first kiss. We had been called to the local supermarket for reports of shop theft. As we made our way knowing I would make the arrest I tried my best to remember the caution by saying it over and over in my mind.

"You do not have to say anything, but it may harm your defence when questioned later something you do not mention and later rely on in court. Anything you do say may be given in evidence"

Although I have seen this typical cop humour version, not quite sure how it would help the general public perception of the police though.

"You have the right to remain motionless, or you may elect to run away from me. Should you decide to run, I shall direct a police dog to chase you down to the ends of the earth. You have the right to have your solicitor run with you. Should he refuse, a trainee solicitor will

be appointed by the court to jog along with you. If while running, you suddenly decide to end the race, beware that a police dog may or may not understand your intentions, and may continue the pursuit and bite you. You may stop running at any time, at your own risk. Good luck. On your mark, get set.... GO!!!!!"

Using that would mean all police officers would have to have a dog. However, it would double police numbers without the need to pay for more police officers, just the odd can of dog food and a few bones.

On arriving at the supermarket, security met us and told us it was a female who they had detained for trying to push a trolley of about £200 worth of shopping straight out the main entrance and to her car. The reason for the attempted theft was for her boyfriend Frank Spencer who was being released from prison the next day.

The woman called Betty, she was in her early fifties and smelt heavily of alcohol. However, as she had not been seen actually driving, we had no grounds to do a roadside breath test. She could have easily turned round and said she had left the car there before having any alcohol, or someone else was going to drive the car home. She may not even be over the limit either. Once I got Betty stood up, I tried my best to deliver the correct caution but my mouth went dry and it all came out completely wrong. I applied handcuffs and we took her to the police car for the short drive to the custody suite.

It is amazing how when faced with a new situation even though you have gone through it and know it, you mind goes totally blank. Even though it had not been perfect I had managed to undertake my first arrest the first of many I hoped my next one would be better, well hopefully…

My next arrest came only a week later and with the same cop. This time the arrest was for criminal damage. A woman called Peggy in her late thirties had kicked her next door neighbour's door during an argument and damaged it. It was all part of an on-going dispute and the women we were going round to the arrest was normally the victim. All though, both sets of neighbours would put complaints and counter allegations into the police. It was all very school ground like behaviour being very tit for tat. The police were basically the stick that one neighbour could use to get beat and get the upper hand on the other. It never ceases to amaze me how childish grown adults can be, all too often the police are in the middle of it.

Why people could not get along sometimes and bury the hatchet is the question I still ask to this day. These disputes often cause an immense amount of stress and unhappiness. But there is always one side that will not let go and these disputes can last for years or until someone gives up or moves house.

Peggy was a little perplexed at being arrested, for me I was just happy to have said the caution faultlessly and the chance to carry out a second arrest. She did not come quietly, but the female cop I was with was excellent at talking and soothing the situation. The way she handled this very disgruntled woman was really good. She was both very professional and assertive. She did not start to raise her voice just spoke in an even tone, and did not rise to the woman's agitated state and threats. She simply explained the situation and what was going to be done. I still use the same technique to this day and even when faced with the arrest of an offender with violence markers, I have found they can still come quietly. All through being treated with respect and spoken to in the right manner.

I recently went to a job that was an on-going issue between a group of boys. One boy had made a flippant remark about cancer and another boy took it personally having just lost and aunt to cancer. From this point, the boy found himself being bullied at school and sometimes chased by the other group. The school also got involved after parental complaints and even though the boy had apologised to everyone involved he was still being chased and bullied. The boy's father Ted Bovis decided to get involved by threatening the lads bullying his son, as the school seemed unable to prevent it. This in turn led to a father of one of the boys storming round to the boy being bullied house were an altercation and tussle on the doorstep took place. Ted who was defending his property decided to get a golf club and hit the other father, Jeffery Fairbrother over the shoulder, causing quite serious bruising. That incident was under investigation by another officer.

A week later after the incident I got called to the boy who was being bullied house with a job of "Violence against others." The job was that a group of lads had just chased him off the local park and threatened him. He had not been injured so was not actually "Violence against others" more anti-social behaviour. I was working with the local PCSO and he knew it was an on-going job so we decided to visit the local park first to see what had transpired. The group directly involved legged it off as the PCSO came up the back path as I drove round to the front but sadly was a little too late. The two we spoke to, said there had been no "chasing" just some shouting of abuse.

In between the call to the police and us arriving at the park, Ted had been out and threatened the kids and asked the other boys involved to have a fight with his son and, "Sort it out." With this we made our way to the house unsure of what to expect really. I started off by asking what had happened and in not too short a time, the parents were getting quite irate. The mother, Gladys was calling the lads "skanks" and other names, which I had to politely and firmly tell her to not use such phrases. The father was making all sorts of threats of what he was going to do to the parents of the boys if we did not sort it. He was no stranger to violence having a record of violence.

With a little bit of good communication and reasoning we were able to calm them down. I knew that we really needed to resolve this situation quickly, as it was a pressure pot about to explode. Meanwhile whilst still at the address, another call and come in from one of the other boys involved parents, complaining of threatening behaviour about the bullied boy's father. I hope you are still keeping up with me and this ever changing story.

We visited the parents of the other boys and spoke directly to them to try to put a lid on things before they got worse. To be fair the other parents were a little shocked by what had been going on as is so often the case with teenagers they only ever tell one half of the story. With that resolved a couple of hours later I was able to speak to the now much calmer Gladys, who was now happy with the way we had sorted everything. I cannot say if it is truly sorted or not, only time will tell. Being a police officer is often being a mediator and problem solver, sometimes the only equipment you need is a functioning brain and good communication.

After that job, I made my way back to the police station and was with a colleague having a cuppa when the radio broke our idle chatter, with reports of a male who was going to kill himself. My colleague knew the lad involved and the family, that would be best described as the type you would find on 'Trisha' quite dysfunctional and plenty of issues. The lad called Arthur had been a menace a few years ago, but having been party to the creation of three children had become less of an issue. Some people really should have a knot tied in it, or a cork pushed up it, as these poor kids end up being dysfunctional themselves, by growing up in an abusive situation. On this occasion Arthur's ex-partner had rang in, to say he had left her a note saying he was going to hang himself in the woods at the edge of the very large village.

Cops were sent in from all angles, probably about 15 of us and the helicopter was on standby. We were tasked with the address of the ex-partner. She told us they had broken up a year ago, then had had an on off relationship. Before she got fed up with his nastiness and told him to get lost and did not want to see him. However, she worked with him at the same shop and allowed him to come and see the three children whenever he wanted. Arthur had left a box with DVDs, passport and various photos of himself at the front door before making off. The letters were quite strongly worded even though the ex said "he is always threatening to kill himself, been doing it for as long as I have known him."

I went and checked the back garden and noticed the back gate went out into a courtyard to some garages that time seemed to have forgotten. About a minute after I got back into the property, the cop who had gone to his home address said he had turned up. Then another minute later she got on the radio out of breath saying he had done a runner. We went to the front of the house and ran down the road. Unbeknown that he had just run back to the garages time had forgot and disappeared. Before the cop chasing him, who had tripped over a wheelie bin during the pursuit had managed to catch up with him. I ran back to the garages and awaited the helicopter, which had now been called in to aid us in our search. By now, all the stars of Jeremy Kyle and Trisha were out on the street, watching cops running in all directions and a police helicopter buzzing overhead. Asking an assortment of questions, whilst swigging on a can of lager. Arthur had now doubled back to the house as the helicopter found him. Before myself, and the female cop who had tried to detain him had got back to the house. We were greeted by a family member, telling us Arthur had just made off again on a bike riding straight past a cop standing on the pavement. The duty Inspector ordered all of us to 'three six' him. This meant arresting under the mental health act, due to the contents of the letters and his behaviour. The helicopter tracked him on his black mountain bike as he sped through the village streets up and down alleyway's thinking he was Bradley Wiggins out for another gold medal.

I spotted him cycling towards me 50 feet away but on seeing me he turned right down yet another alleyway with cops in pursuit. This chase was becoming more and more like the 'Keystone cops' or possibly a Benny Hill chase going round in circles. He was finally arrested, funnily enough just outside of the local police station and taken a mental health unit. Half of the village was now on the street watching the entertainment and every few yards I got asked what was going on. I was struggling to breathe let alone talk after a little too much exercise for my liking.

PDR

During my first Performance Development Review or PDR for short, the sergeant decided to take a light hearted stance, whilst going through the checklist on what I was competent at. He then had to give a grade for each one, one, two or three. Whilst going through the checklist, he decided to tell me an old police tale to make the proceeding more purposeful. The story was about a job when two cops had been sent to deal with a rather drunk elderly gentleman found strewn in the street. He was propped up against a fence, just under a street lamp. He sat there mumbling quite incoherent, unable to move such was the intoxicated state he was in. One of the officers did a quick check of his pockets for a wallet or some form of ID. Thankfully, they found some ID and an address, as the choice was to arrest him for being drunk and incapable or the far less paper heavy option of taking him home. Such was his intoxicated state that he was unable to stand unaided and it took two burly police officers had to literally drag him to a police car. The elderly gentleman, now known as Basil Faulty, at least cam quietly and then fell asleep in the back of the police car on the way home. Apparently, he used to own a rather bad hotel but was now retired.

Finally, back at Basil's address a woman opened the door and introduced herself as Cybil, stood just behind her was the lodger they currently had, who was from Spain. As the two police officers dragged Basil into the house and sat him on the lounge. Cybil piped up and said, "Where is his wheelchair?" The two police officers looked at one another and knew they were now dealing with a theft.

Unsure of quite how that story fitted in with my PDR, my sergeant then said, "Never assume anything." I thought that was quite cunning to integrate a relevant story into my PDR, which fitted in with an assumption I had made a couple of weeks previous. I was sent to a job of a burglary in progress, which meant as many units as possible were being sent all on blue lights. A call had come in of Bill and Ben, known career criminals seen undertaking their next burglary. These two seemed to be able to dodge the law at every turn and would steal anything, including a flower pot it was not nailed down. Bill and Ben were both quite weedy in terms of their build and stature, but boy could they run. Not one of us were able to catch them on foot, not helped by the weight of our equipment, compared to their shell suit and matching Nike trainers. Determined to catch them in the act or at least with the loot, we ensured that we all came in from different directions to have the best chance of cutting off their escape route. It was all sadly to no avail, Bill and Ben and yet again slipped off into the night. In some ways, I was grateful, as Bill and Ben were street savvy and would often use the law against police officers. One such trick was to spit on their hands and then wipe this onto the face or the hands of an unsuspecting cop. This DNA transfer could then be used as evidence later to say they had been hit by a police officer. They have nearly got two police officers sacked for excessive use of force using this trick. Which apparently had come from Eastern Europe, where it had become quite a common tactic, or so I have been told.

I was first at the scene of the reported burglary, and to be honest the house was such a mess it looked like nothing had been taken. I did a quick tour of the house with the occupant, a very nice woman called Ivana Steal. Her house had so many boxes that her house looked more like a warehouse than anything else. She said that nothing had been taken and I was happy to of battered that job off and not taken on any paperwork. A week later, the house was raided by CID, they had been working on a burglary and fencing ring for a couple of months and Ivana Steal was at the centre of it. When Ivana's house was raided, it was found to be full to the brim of stolen items that I had missed. Bill and Ben who had been seen leaving the house had actually gone to drop stuff off. Two months later Bill and Ben were finally caught red handed about to break into a garden shed and had a little weed stashed in their pockets. Ivana turned vegetarian inside and changed her name to Ivana Trumpalot, quite apt with her new found love of Brussels sprouts!

Operation

The local area Inspector had got a real bee in his bonnet about several new bars that had opened, and wanted regular patrols every Friday and Saturday night in the town centre. For the most part, it was not too bad for us in response, but the poor special's had to endure week after week of walking around doing the same thing. I dare say it did become rather tiresome and a bit boring for them. I personally have always enjoyed foot patrol, although most hate it. However, for me what I like most about being a cop is the variety and working with different cops and agencies is a good way of networking and getting useful information and contacts.

The offshoot from the bar patrols, was the local area Inspector wanted an operation checking vehicles, especially taxis. An operation was set up in my division to check car's for a whole variety of offences. From the vehicle condition to road tax and insurance checks, this was my first real operation. The operation for once was very well planned, we had a vehicle inspector, DVLA and custom and excise officers joining us. The custom and excise officers were joining us to test for anyone using red diesel. So called as a red dye was added to denote it was for agricultural use and fuel duty had not been paid for it.

The operation went well at first; we alternated stopping cars in pairs as the young in service were put with more experienced cops. We did hand out a few tickets for not wearing a seatbelt, using mobile phones and various vehicle defects. One car was seized for having no tax or insurance. It went well at first, until the weather took a change for the worst and it started to rain and then rain even harder. I had not brought all my waterproofs so after an hour in the rain; I probably would have been drier if I had jumped into a swimming pool fully clothed. Believe me, soggy wet underpants is not a nice way to sit down and be comfortable. The cold also started to eat away at me and I started to shiver. Thankfully, the rain made the management decide to finish early, and we headed back to the police station for tea and medals. In my case, some dry clothes and home to a nice hot bath.

One of the big shocks with the police, especially at uniform level is how reactive everything is. If a group of houses gets burgled, extra patrols are pumped into that area just in case the naughty people come back. Being PC A Hole, I usually get shafted, and end up patrolling one of the areas that has just been hit. Whilst the burglars complete with swag bags that in our modern times have evolved into wheelie bins. They dash about with their wheelie bins full of loot, and if spotted just leaving the wheelie bin next to a house. Who would think to check a wheelie bin for loot?

Whilst everyone is focused on one area, another area becomes a crime hot spot and so on. Lack of manpower is one theory or just the need to target hot spots and reduce crime. Being proactive in many cases would solve the situation. Only last month a beat team got put on an operation in a different area. Even though they protested that really they should be patrolling their own area it fell on deaf ears.

The long and short of it was that their area had a spate of burglaries, whilst they were on the operation. So the next weekend they were once again being reactive, patrolling the same area where the burglaries had taken place. This is the current nature of the beast, and with government targets to meet with reduced manpower. There are not many options for management to choose, so being reactive is something that will continue for years. I am however hopeful that the new crime commissioners can take the battle back to the government. Now they have seen directly how the funding cuts are affecting the level of service the public receive. It is only down to the hard working and dedicated cop's, up and down the country that anarchy has not started to set in.

First Couple of Years

After finishing my initial probation, I suppose I started one of my happiest times in the police. I was quickly approaching three years of service. Those three years seemed to have flown by, I had learnt allot, but still had much to learn, the odd new cop joined the shift and a whole host of new specials after a big recruitment drive. Sadly most of those recruited subsequently quit and the retention rate for special's has never managed to get above 40% with most leaving during their first two years of service. Last year 1400 Specials were recruited across the country and 1700 left. The current number of serving specials stands at just over 19,000.

Specials are lucky in some respects though as they can decide when they want to come on duty and when they want to go home. Professionally, though many would not just decide to go off duty in the middle of an arrest or operation. You do get some interesting people passing through recruitment to become specials. Sometimes it has been the case that they were totally unsuitable to be a cop. One that springs to mind is SC Lame, a really nice chap but if you asked him to detain someone whilst you did some checks. By the time you had come back, the detained person had done a runner. He had no communication ability what so ever. He moved closer to where he lived so he could stay on until 10pm, however that did not work out either and he left. Another Special called SC Breadbin, a baker by day, who had not long been recruited, turned out to have some rather dodgy links to local crime families and was told to resign. He would have been a great cop if he only used his loaf... sorry bad joke.

More recently quite an unpleasant special SC Hazard took one of the smaller vans out and the roof lights collided with a height restrictor at a local park ripping the lights off. Rather than come clean and admit fault and probably get a good bollocking. He decided to say the lights had fallen off on a rough section of road. The special he was with also backed up this story. Sadly they both had to resign due to lack of integrity as it was proved that the lights had been ripped off, not fallen off. The special that was not driving came clean about what had actually happened the next day, but it was too late and his integrity was in tatters. To be honest, anyone looking at the lights could see it was impossible for them to just "bounce off" after going over a large bump. SC Hazard had been tutored by another maverick special that was known for cutting corners and getting himself into scrapes.

This special had all the makings of a good cop; he just needed to calm down a bit. On one occasion, he was out on a plain clothes operation with another special. When they came across two sixteen year old females who were quite intoxicated. Somehow, these two females ended up assaulting them and one apparently had their hands round his neck so he used CS spray on them. How you could get yourself in that situation, in the first place I will never know. I would have got uniformed backup if they had not wanted to recognise me as a cop, due to not being in uniform. He managed to get himself into another force as a full-timer and I am sure with the right training and a tight leash will become an excellent cop. It was felt he would either be seriously injured or sacked by many of the full-time cops. So far in my career I must have seen at least twenty specials come and go in my area alone.

Anyway back to my happy times… I worked with a shift that both worked hard and were also allot of fun to work with. The banter and practical jokes were pretty funny and usually aimed at cops from other shifts. One cop who would always moan about the state of the police car's after our shift had used them. Was left at the end of our shift one day with Wotsits crushed up all over the driver's seat, and then various empty wrappers and cans that we had found were strewn across the back seat. There was the temptation to leave a dog turd in the footwell, but we felt that might be going a little too far, even if the cop concerned was a right pain in the arse.

During my happy time there seemed to be a real surge of anti-social behaviour (ASB) type incidents, as our area seemed flooded with teenagers up to no good. Although, those up to no good was a small minority.

Time after time, I have explained to young people how the world now portrays them, with their hoodies on and in large groups, many people find them intimidating. As soon as the public sees a group of hoodies they assume they must be up to no good, which nine times out of ten is not true. Teenagers just need somewhere to go and be teenagers. Experience has taught me most are actually alright, you can have a chat and a bit of banter. Most, once the reasons are explained will actually do as requested. Of course you always get the more hardened "show off" type that want to prove to their mates they can get one over on the, "Feds" the current street name for the police.

They're the ones I usually go for and make life difficult, one arrest or a hefty fine has an amazing effect on the others. They usually start to wind their necks in pretty quick. Over the years, I have found ASB seems to come in waves, a group starts off silly and slowly moves up the ASB scale until they either grow up, get into girls or get locked up for more serious offences. The wave passes and you maybe get a couple of years' respite before the next wave comes along. An area can go years without trouble, then all of a sudden you get a wave of ASB incidents that seem to last for one to two years before vanishing as quickly as they started.

Some more notable incidents I attended during my 'happy times' was for an attempted burglary at a local primary school. I was with a beat manger from my station and we made our way to the scene. The police dogs and helicopter had been called as the offenders had been seen running away from the scene. The helicopter was soon on scene and could not locate or see anything. I had just climbed over a wall when I got shouted at to get out as the police dog was being put over the wall. The dog's make no distinction between the offender and a police officer. As soon as the dog got in it started barking as it had found the first suspect. I had been less than two metres away from him when the dog was let in. The helicopter went off to its next call a few miles away, whilst a cop on the ground located the second suspect.

The final and strange job I attended that night was a concern for safety. A worried family could not get hold of their daughter, even though they believed she was in her flat. We were given permission to kick the down and go looking for her. There was no sign of her initially and the flat was in total darkness. The bathroom door was locked and as I tried it, I heard a scream come from the bathroom. So I forced the white panelled bathroom door open, to find her semi naked. On trying to open the door I had awoken her, somewhat relieved. She had got herself locked in the bathroom without her mobile phone, and spent a night on the towels.

I regularly worked with the same cop and we became not only good friends but a good team as well. When you are sitting beside someone for maybe ten hours at a time you do get to know them really well, after all you probably spend more time with them than you do with your own family. You learn how to almost second judge what each other will do next and just one look is all it takes to know what each other is thinking.

He later decided to go and work in CID which was a great loss for both the shift and myself.

Downturn

With the loss of my partner, I did feel somewhat lost; we had spent nearly every night shift working together for three years. Now being a tutor constable myself, I had a couple of new special constables to tutor one who ended up freezing on her second shift out after we became surrounded by about 25 youths. Freezing is all too easy when placed into a stressful situation and you do not know what to do. At my first big incident, I froze momentarily but with time and experience you don't freeze. You tend to assess the situation and quickly formulate a plan of action or use your instincts. On this occasion, even though I knew there was no one available to back us up, I still shouted it over the radio, just so the kids thought help was on its way. This did help to get some of the youths to disperse slowly.

With my student officer standing very quiet and motionless, I decided the only other course of action was to go for the ringleader, aptly named Robin Hood. Although, he stole from the local shop to feed himself. Due to not being able to afford a boob job, he had decided the best way to get love handles was to stuff a few king sized Snickers in his gob.

Robin Hood was doing his best to try to run me over on his trusty steed, a black BMX in his fetching green hoodie with the hood up. I hauled him off his bike by his hood and detained him. He tried his best to protest and act the little John, but being threatened with being arrested or taken home along with a few words to his parents meant he begrudgingly backed down along with his band of merry men . Not without the immortal words "PIG" being shouted when they thought, they were at a safe distance from us.

The special with me, had all the makings of a good special, but she lasted less than a year after a change of job and having just got engaged changed her mind. I also felt that she decided being a cop was not for her either. To be fair what people see on the TV is not really an accurate picture of what can happen or how people will feel when they are actually dealing with the serious accident, dead body or violent criminal. As said and I will say it again, police work is more often than not hours of nothing followed by 10 minutes of action and 4 hours of paperwork. Any new recruit is shocked with the amount of paperwork, that usually dawns on them in training school, when they endure a 91 page PowerPoint presentation on who to create a prosecution file for the CPS.

After a few years, I felt as a cop, I was starting to get bored and lose my enthusiasm for the job; I did start to consider changing careers or maybe even re-training to do something very different. The big issue was my salary, and that I may well have to take a pay drop from my current salary at the time of about £28,000. Something Mrs Hole was not too happy with, especially with another little Hole on the way.

I just rode my bad time out, and threw myself into various training courses including public order training. Just so I could spend some time with the PSU (Police Support Unit) doing raids or working football matches. It did help to break up the routine of being a response cop and going to similar incidents with a different flavour time after time.

At the same time, I had another student officer SC Amanda Hug 'n' Kiss who I thought was turning out to be ok. I was not quite sure of their intentions or reasons to join. However, the first couple of months went OK. She started to date a married cop and moved in together. Sadly, this was doomed to failure, the cop in question was quite hot tempered and rumours of domestic violence began to surface. This cop always managed to annoy and wind up people with his manner and what I thought at times was unprofessional behaviour, that myself and other cops would challenge. In the end we are a public service and here to serve. Everyone deserves to be treated with respect, there are those members of the public that no amount of politeness will change their view or hostility towards the police. If you remain calm and polite yourself, at least the perception of the public around you is unlikely to be negative and they are more likely to understand the situation. With so much social media, any incident especially if handled badly is on various sites within seconds. They say that people that have had a bad experience of a service, will tell 9-10 people. Those that have had a good experience will tell 2-3 people.

SC Amanda Hug 'n' Kiss was quite wound up about the situation with about the cop she was currently dating and living with, along with how badly he was treating her. As we pulled up to a set of traffic lights, I noticed a group of men jostling and shoving each other at the side of a pub. As soon as the lights changed to green, I made my way round to the front of the pub and parked up. I leapt out the car just as I saw a man in a grey jumper hit another man. I raced over without really thinking or even getting on my radio to inform control that a fight was taking place.

I rushed in and tried to arrest the man who had just thrown the punch, as I went to make the arrest by grabbing his arm and tell him what I was arresting him for, his mates started to surround me and persuade me not to arrest him. The man protested his innocence and said he had done nothing wrong. As I started to pull him away, his mates started to pull him in the other direction and this led to me being pulled to the floor. Realising I was not in a good position I hit the orange panic button on my radio and due to the surrounding noise screamed my need for assistance; making half the police officers on shift deaf.

My student officer to her credit shouted at everyone to back off and I got up onto my feet. By now, I had been joined by two other specials and had my baton drawn as I got everyone to back off. Another woman kicked one of the specials in the knee as that special tried to move the crowd back. By now, cops were coming in at all angles. One by one various people were being arrested and led away. I pointed out the man who I had tried to arrest originally and he was arrested. One male who we have talked to normally one minute ended on the floor the next, after he suddenly lashed out at another cop. Armed response had arrived were assisting us arrest the man who had tried to hit another cop and was now quite a handful. Slowly we managed to gain control and get him into the small police car I was driving.

Once in custody the man I had tried to arrest initially was being booked in. If looks could kill, he would have done me in. Not a happy chap, especially with yours truly. The male I was booking in, had now calmed down and was behaving himself. In the end, 25 cops had come to my aid. The question of could it be handled did occur both in my mind and the minds of others I am sure. The answer to that question is a resounding yes. I needed to talk more and taken action much later, maybe getting other cops on the scene first to kill things. The male, who had been hit, may not have wanted to make a complaint anyway.

I took some ribbing for that job, I had taken the eye off the ball and got distracted by the special constable I was trying to support and tutor.

I did learn many lessons from that incident; I had also created an awful lot of paperwork in terms of witness statements, seized CCTV and everything else that was needed. Including the use of force form, that had to be filled out every time we used any force.

The second cock up, was only two months later when I was on foot patrol SC Amanda Hug 'n' Kiss. We were walking through the park when ahead I saw two males;

one of the males was smoking. As he saw us, he threw something to his side. As we got closer, I could still smell cannabis on his breath. With that I had grounds to search for drugs, which I duly did and came up with nothing.

As I took his details, he crouched down and picked up the nub end of the joint he had been smoking and asked me what he should do with it. In a moment of madness, I told him to throw it in the bin, not realising it still contained cannabis. Firstly it was grounds to issue a cannabis warning as the man had been smoking and still reeked of cannabis. Secondly I was asking him to discard the evidence. In my effort to cut corners I was soon to realise, I had landed myself in hot water. I told the beat manager for the area, what I had done and whilst not impressed, realised it was an unintentional mistake. SC Amanda Hug 'n' Kiss had for some reason decided she would inform my Inspector. Two weeks later, I was in the Inspector's office for a right telling off. My sergeant thought it was all bang out of order and came to my defence. As for SC Amanda Hug 'n' Kiss she was pretty much ostracised by the regular cops, although I continued to tutor her for a short while longer, whilst she completed her tutoring period. After that, my sergeant actually told her he did not want her working with his shift. She continued as a special for a further two years working every now and again before leaving. Not many months after that incident, I dealt with a job that did affect me strangely and played on my mind for months. It was not that I had actually seen anything horrific, more the thoughts of what could have been.

I was sent to a job, which was dealing with the attempted murder of a baby and GBH. I was the only resource available even though armed response had been called. A male who was separated from his girlfriend had tried to snatch his own baby, and in doing so started to crush it and pull it. He had turned up to his ex-partner's house in quite intoxicated and had driven there in his drunken state. After forcing his way in and beating his ex-partner up a neighbour had come round to help out and they had then also been beaten up. He grabbed the baby intentionally trying to crush it, before deciding to put it in a carrycot to take it away. As his ex-partner screamed at him to leave and another neighbour shouted that the police had been called. He did no less than throw the baby in its carrycot at his ex-partner. It missed her and crashed on the floor with the baby still strapped in. Before he stormed out the house got into his car and drove off.

Amazingly, the baby was uninjured, his ex- girlfriend had severe bruising to the face and the neighbour had some slight bruising to their face. I followed the ambulance to the hospital after taking initial details and waiting for some full-time officers to come to my aid. It was one of those jobs that made me think, "Where the hell do I start?" With multiple IP's and witnesses, it was a big job and I felt my bottom twitch at the thought of what I was dealing with. On arrival, the ambulance was already there, the offender had not been picked up by armed response, who was trying to locate him. I needed advice on what they wanted me to do next. This was also at shift change over so getting through to the night shift sergeant took a little while. Finally, when the response sergeant got in touch, he said to go to the hospital and take details of any injuries and take photos of any injuries.

I ended up feeling almost overwhelmed by everything that had gone on and what the offender had done. At the same time, it left me drained. I have never been to a job since that has had such a profound effect on me.

Time for a Change

After another two years, I decided it was time for a change and wanted to move stations. There was a rationale to it all though. I was totally honest with my shift sergeant, and told him that I was a little fed up and wanted a change. Also coupled with wanting to be closer to where I lived. He put the request through, minus wanting to be nearer home. I was lucky that there was a vacant position in the area I wanted to move to, which meant my transfer request was accepted.

I did my final shift, on foot for a plain clothed operation. It was supposed to be a covert operation, although trying to look covert whilst wearing a stab vest and arrest equipment beneath your coat was no easy task. By chance, I was with my old student officer SC Amanda Hug 'n' Kiss, whom I was still suspicious of. She looked none too pleased to be working with me, but I cannot say I was that keen either. I could not fathom the reason she had it in for me, but then that is life and I was not going to let her bother me. The operation was to walk round the burglary hotspots keeping a keen eye out for any naughty people, especially those pulling a wheelie bin!

I had four days off before moving to my new station and response team. This team had just two other cops and the sergeant was based at another station with another three cops to look after. We were free of direct supervision and the usual shift briefing, although we always had a quick chat and look at the various briefings and tasking systems before going out on patrol. I work with PC Shore, who is great when needing to make a decision at an incident and then there is PC Wellliked, who gets on with everybody with his positive manner and courteous nature.

We also had a special, SC Dallas who was a real character even if a bit of a liability working every Friday night. I often ended up taking him out with me as felt sorry for him as the other cops seemed to avoid him. The special I worked with knew the area really well as he only lived down the road from the Police station. He was originally from America and still had an American accent, which was the source of much amusement to the other cops. Especially when he came on the radio with American phrases. Such as, "I am on the Apex to church street" said in his broad Texan accent. He was in his early sixties and boy could he talk and talk. Even on the radio he would almost tell everyone on the same channel what he was thinking. On one occasion, he found a male strewn out on his back in a pub car park. First, he announced, "He is dead" then "Oh he moved, he is not dead just unconscious" and finally "Oh he is conscious just very drunk". In between all of this control was trying to get him to tell them if an ambulance was required or not.

However, he was the nicest person you could wish to meet and would do anything for anyone. He was great with handling of victims of crime and was so nice people would invite him in for a cup of tea and a chat. His problem area was police procedure and knowledge of the law. He would often get himself in a pickle through lack of knowledge. He really should not be out on his own, but no one wanted to work with him. His problems were made worse by not being tutored properly in the first place before being let out on his own.

The stories of him trying to arrest innocent people or give out wrong tickets were numerous. One time I was dealing with a drink driver and struggling to put the handcuffs on. Instead of leaping in to help me, he just got on the radio to tell them I was struggling. The guy was totally obnoxious towards me and made every threat and said every expletive towards me. SC Dallas being the nice bloke he was, still offered to give him a lift home after we had processed and charged him with drink driving.

We attended a couple of RTCs, and he was really good with me just telling him what to do and where to go. One in particular was quite nasty when a car had clipped the low curb on the bend of a 60mph single carriageway and then somersaulted into the air and ended up upside down in a ditch. The car was in a bad way and when we got there, the fire brigade was in attendance as was an ambulance. The male driving the car had been very lucky indeed and managed to drag himself out of the car. All he had suffered was a broken collarbone and a severely bruised leg along with some minor cuts and bruises.

SC Dallas's other problem was the ability to wind up management. He was very outspoken and not in a bad way. He said what everyone else thought but knew it was not the always best thing to say. He complained about poor leadership and training opportunities. All of this did not help him to win anyone over. They tried to get rid of him for two years, but without much luck, before finally forcing him to retire. In a couple of interviews with management, he had a recording pen he got in America, and used it to record the meeting for future evidence. Adding further to the annoyance management had with him. They finally got rid of him by forcing him to retire.

With him gone I was back to being on my own any Friday night I worked, as they did not want us to double crew to ensure the maximum number of cars out patrolling . Although after years of mainly being double crewed I did enjoy being single crewed, I liked the freedom and the ability to plan my patrol and then respond to jobs as they came in. Within the first year I got two good arrests for cannabis, several drink drivers and a couple of arrests for shoplifting. The cannabis collars always required backup though, as the first was two up. I had followed a car for driving erratically and subsequently pulled it over. On opening the door, I was hit with a large and a strong waft of cannabis smoke that was being smoked by the passenger, but had affected the driver. I then requested backup, and undertook some checks done whilst I waited for backup. Being in a rural location, backup could take 15-20 minutes. Therefore, you had to be a little more cautious and handle situations well. It ended with a good arrest and a cannabis warning being issued.

The second cannabis collar was a little funnier in a way. I drove past a car pulled up on a gravel layby next to a railway line. The car was parked in the middle of nowhere between two small villages. As I went past they clocked me, looking suspicious I went past and turned round a bit further down the road. The car with the four people in it made off. I planned to catch them up at road speed, just so I could get the registration for intelligence use. At that point, I had no intention of putting the blue lights on and pulling them over. Anyhow, the driver decided to indicate and pull over on his own accord. When I asked why he had pulled over he said I had flashed my headlights at him, when in reality it was that the road was a bit bumpy causing my headlights to bounce up and down slightly, giving the effect I was flashing my headlights.

Again, the car reeked of cannabis and being four up, I called for backup and kept everyone in the car less the driver. Everyone else in the car was underage and when the other cop searched the car he found a small bag that contained cannabis or green vegetable matter as we always put on the seizure form until it was tested and verified to be cannabis. PC Wellhung came to my aid and we searched and found a very small amount of cannabis.

The same cop, PC Beef was also with me when a call came in from Ambulance of a male they were having difficulty with. As I got on scene I could see the two distinctive green uniforms of the paramedics and a scruffy looking male in blue tracksuit bottoms and a grey top staggering across the road. As I got to him, I was joined by a colleague and we did our best to talk to him. But he was totally out of it; the ambulance crew believed he was having some type of seizure connected to his diabetes. He tried to get away from us and back into a busy main road. We had no choice but to get him onto the floor. Such was his strength we needed to handcuff him but could not get both arms close enough together and were forced to use two sets of handcuffs. We then performed a ground pin, with me on his legs and the other cop on his shoulders, whilst waiting for the fit to pass, so the paramedics could treat him. He had the strength of an ox and PC Beef, unlike PC Hole, is very muscular and well built. He was struggling to control him as he got on top of the male. PC Beef used to be a builder before joining the force, specialising in conservatory erections.

With the fit over, I stood up to an unpleasant smell and looked down at my trouser to notice they were covered in human excrement. During the fight, the man had lost control of his bowels and deposited the contents over my trousers and the tip of my asp. I travelled in the ambulance with him and as he came round, he could not remember anything of what had just occurred. He was a lovely chap as we got chatting on our way to the hospital, you would not believe it was the same man who had been grunting and struggling with us 10 minutes previously.

PC Beef later told the rest of the shift with some delight; in usual cop banter how he had got me in the shit, quite literally.

Another strange job in similar circumstances was when an ambulance was taking a woman into hospital and as they were travelling, she tried to jump out of the back of the ambulance at 60mph. The woman was known to us, as we regularly got called to her house for various self-harm attempts, which normally consisted of stuffing razor blades up her vagina.

I was on my own so another unit was also dispatched. On arrival the woman was at the side of the road next to the ambulance, I tried my best to cajole her back into the ambulance, but the minute I tried to move her she started to fight. I had no choice, but to pin her down on the floor whilst another cop handcuffed her. With the handcuffs on, I got her onto the bed in the back of the ambulance, and sat on her until we got to the hospital. The cop with me said, "I doubt she will be able to sit down for weeks if that razor blade slices those girly bits. Faster than a speeding bullet and sharper than a razor I replied, "I doubt it either; she had initially called us to report her sofa had been stolen." The actuality was that she had been burgled it seemed, and the burglar had taken two antique chairs. The whole burglary turned out to be a rubbish job, she had thrown the chairs in a skip and nothing else had been stolen.

At the hospital, I had to remove the handcuffs, as the hospital would not admit anyone wearing handcuffs. She had calmed down and the ambulance guys were able to get inside her, I mean get her inside. We stayed inside for a bit longer just in case, but she seemed perfectly calm and relaxed.

RTC's are the mainstay of the work I carry out being more rural. The mixture of 60mph roads that should not really be 60 and poor weather conditions often lead to some quite nasty crashes. Some that have looked like the people should not have survived but have survived the crash without a mark on them. Only last week I went to an RTC where a car had gone too far over the centre line and a van had swerved to try to avoid it. Being a very wet night the van had spun round and hit the car he was trying to avoid before ending up in a ditch. The elderly gentleman in the car had been drinking although only blew 30 which meant he was just under the limit of 35. He got a good telling off from me as I suspect that his wandering across the centre line had everything to do with alcohol as the poor weather conditions. I felt sorry for the driver of the van who had only just brought the van, as two weeks earlier someone had covered both his wife's car and his van in paint stripper, and written them both off.

Another more serious RTC I attended was a few months back, which I literally stumbled upon. An ambulance was already in attendance, and I could see a newish Ford Fiesta sitting in a front garden. The car had crossed over onto the other side of the road after swerving on a bend before hitting a concrete pillar on the drive way, and t-boning a tree. The passenger side of the car was totally gone and mangled, if a passenger had been present they would have most likely be killed. The female driver was already out and on a spinal board; she looked in a bad way and was slipping in and out of consciousness. Due to the severity of the accident, we had to close the road, and then I stood on the same road until about 1am when I was relived. The process of accident investigation is a slow and thorough one that can take hours. We have a special unit that goes to all serious or fatal accidents and they took charge of the scene and investigation.

The women survived after being in a coma for three days, the cause of the crash was excessive speed and a slightly damp road causing her to lose control on the bend, even though it was a 40mph limit she had been doing over 50mph. It was not the first crash on this stretch of road many of the residents had had cars pay a visit to their gardens at one time or another over the past few years.

We also have a main line railway station in the area I cover and often get called to thefts or fights on the station. Although once I was called to a local railway station that was on a busy main line with reports of a man who had been hit by a train. Obvious first thoughts I had was, "was he dead?" It was only a good 5 minutes' drive from our location so a PCSO and I made our way there. The response sergeant was first on the scene, he reported it in as a man lying beside the railway line conscious and breathing but with serious injuries. As we arrived, the ambulance had just arrived and British Transport Police (BTP) pulled in behind us. Being a railway line, it was actually BTP jurisdiction, so we were there to support until BTP took over responsibility. One thing that struck me first was that the man was lying on the far opposite of the tracks from where the train had stopped.

The other thing that surprised me when I went to see the station manager about the best route to get the casualty out was that the tracks were still live. This meant that trains had not been stopped, I suggested she should close the line. This section of the line was a 70mph section with fast express trains flying through and several cops right next to and on the railway line. Another cop was helping to deal with the male who had obviously had a compound fracture to his arm a very large dent in his forehead, his mouth and chest was also covered in blood. The air ambulance was also called in and more paramedic units continued to arrive. The response sergeant for my area had found about £1500 lying on the railway line. The BTP cops who now numbered four said they had come from another station that had had a report of a male hitching a lift on the back of a freight train. It soon became apparent that he had not been hit by a train at all. Nevertheless, he had jumped off the back of a moving freight train and landed left arm then chest first onto the aggregate by the side of the tracks before hitting his head with some force onto the concrete slabs that cover where the line side cables run. BTP reckons the freight train would have been travelling at about 40mph. It turned out that BTP had tried to arrest him at another station and even sprayed him with CS before he had jumped on the back of a moving freight train and made off. They were unsure if he was high on drink or drugs.

The air ambulance arrived and its doctor got the male stable before moving him. By now there were four paramedics including a senior manager to oversee health and safety. Three crew from the air ambulance four BTP and three local cops including myself. Trains were now stacked up either side of the station so quite a bit of disruption for one male who decided it was a good idea to hitch a lift and then jump off a moving train. In the end, after we had got the male across the tracks on a stretcher he was taken to the local hospital by road with two of the air ambulance crew in the back. Sadly, the male died the next morning in hospital.

As BTP had taken responsibility for the incident, I was now free to leave and deal with the next call of a minor RTC that was accident only, involving two cars on a residential street. Both drivers were slightly annoyed with one another, hence the police being called. I quickly calmed the situation down, although I think that was more to my presence as a police officer than anything to do with my oh so fabulous communication ability! Everything was quickly sorted and I could get back to the police station to do another accident card before going state 11 (police speak for going off duty).

Government Cut's

2011 started with the end of a very cold winter. As I said at the start of the book PC Cold is as good as PC Rain for keeping criminals inside. Spring came along, and the burglaries started in a couple of villages in my area. Extra patrols were put in place both on foot and in a car to try and stem the flow. It seemed like they were going from one village to the next. We got a lucky break when we got the getaway car registration number from a witness. They had come across the border from another county to commit burglary and then bug out quickly. The times have been usually late afternoon early evening. By chance, a unit from the other county that the car was from spotted it and pulled it over. Items that they had stolen were still present in the car. Then during an interview, the gang of four admitted to most of the burglaries on our patch and the burglaries ceased for a while.

Being spring, the young people were spending more and more time outside, and with it came the usual ASB, although not that bad. I came on duty one weekend on my own to an email warning me of a possible large fight between two schools in the area.

The park was packed with about 50 youths that I waded into and laid down the riot act. I got some back chat, but most listened to what I would do if there was any disorder. I told them that £80 fines for public order and arrests would rise along with a 24 hour dispersal order to the most troublesome individuals. I said I would have every cop available joining me if necessary. It had the desired effect and they dispersed.

Two hours later, I got a call from a local about youths congregating near to a factory on a country road. I made my way out towards them only to find the same 50 youths all stood in a layby, most probably still waiting for the fight that never happened

Being a section of 60mph road, I pulled in and put the blue lights on. Then one of the youths had the audacity to complain the light was hurting their eyes. Hearing the commotion as I radioed through details, control asked if I needed anyone else. At that time I was ok, although having the potential to get hairy. I told them to move on and again they listened much to my amazement. However, their idea was to walk down the road with the odd one shouting "pig". Not just walk down the side of the road, actually take up half of the road as they walked en-mass.

I tried my best to cajole them to the side of the road then came to a lovely young lady. As I grabbed her arm to move her to the edge of the road, I got told to "fuck off" and to leave her alone. She then said I should not be touching her because she was pregnant! Surely if you are pregnant you do not walk in the middle of a 60mph road or go nearly a mile out of the village on foot, or maybe I am missing something here? She continued to be abusive, so with concern for her safety I was just about to arrest her and take her home. When a friend bundled her into a car and made off, leaving me to deal with the 50 youths walking in the middle of the road. I then radioed for backup and the cavalry was on its way.

I had no choice but to follow at very slow walking speed behind the group, with my blue lights on to protect them from potentially fast moving traffic or causing an accident. I followed them for about half a mile until they went into a bus stop. Some carried on walking and some hung around. As I got out of the car, the same pregnant girl started mouthing off at me again. She got a good talking to, and threatened with an £80 disorder fine. By now, the cavalry had arrived in the form of three Police cars and this was enough to disperse everyone and end any more issues that night.

The PCSO I sometimes work with in my area knew the pregnant girl very well, and told me she was a nasty piece of work. He had had several run in's with her before being pregnant along with the prospect of becoming a mother had not mellowed her at all.

Most Friday and Saturday nights as the weather picked up, I would often find myself going from job to job to job. One Saturday night I had already dealt with a few anti-social jobs when I got called out to an abandoned car on a country lane and was deemed to be in a dangerous position. The car was quite an old purple Vauxhall Astra; it was taxed had an MOT and insurance to view, the owner lived two miles down the road. It had either broken down or run out of petrol. The car was a bit strange in that a pair of black knickers was holding the front windscreen wipers down and on the bike seat was a box that contained some women's clothing including some purple high-heeled shoes black tights and what looked like a dress.

Control tried to get hold of the owner, but to no avail so due to its location, I had no choice but to request it was recovered. That would cost them an £80 release fee. Far better, the car was removed than someone crashing into the back of it during the early hours; such was its dangerous position. It only took the duty garage 20 minutes to arrive and start to recover the car, which was a good job as I had been requested to go to an immediate or red job with reports of a burglary in progress at a business premises some three miles away. I could not go until the car had been fully recovered and no other units were available as the others were already tied up with other jobs.

I made my way to the burglary and sure enough, the burglars had ripped down the front gates and smashed their way through the glass front door. On inspection all I could see stolen was an LCD TV from the reception area.

The owners of the business lived next door, although they were away for the weekend and had left their teenage daughter in charge. She was at university and was looking after her brother and the few mates he had invited round. They were all understandably a little scared, so I reassured them and did all the relevant paperwork. I stayed with them for about an hour, then left but promised that I would drive by their house whilst I was still on duty. Also arrange for the night shift to drive by during the night if they could.

On the owners return they put a complaint in against the police in the poor response time, even though rural areas were given 20 minute response time compared to the 10 for urban areas. I never heard what happened to the complaint although it was no reflection on me as I got there as quickly as I could with full blues and two's.

Being a police officer means that unlike a 9-5 job that you can just turn your computer off and go home, we cannot do that. It is a 24hour service that operates 365 days a year. If you are unlucky enough to get sent to an incident just before you are due to go off may well mean a much later finish than expected. My record is 12 hours later than I was due to finish. One example was when I was driving back to the police station to finish of paperwork and go home. I came up behind a Vauxhall Astra that was weaving slightly and I thought, "Drink driver". It did go through my mind should I just; 'ignore it' as knew that I had no chance of finishing on time if they proved to be over the limit.

To ignore it would be dereliction of duty; I would like to think I am very professional. So when safe to do so I pulled the car over and a petite woman struggling to walk, on very high heeled platform shoes got out of the car. How the devil she could drive in 13cm heels I will never know, Mrs Hole cannot even walk in such high heels let alone drive. As for myself, I nearly crashed the one and only time I tried to drive in flip flops in my younger years, I bet you thought I was about to say heels!

It is amazing how your instinct as a cop clicks in, and I knew the chances of her blowing over the limit were very high indeed. Sure enough she blew 45, so I promptly arrested her and took her to custody. It was 1:50am and I was due to get off at 2am, which was not going to happen now.

I did have some empathy with the woman, as she explained she had been due to stay at her friend's house. They had fallen out after an argument and she was now stranded with no way of getting home. Although, she did admit she could have got her boyfriend to pick her up, but did not want to hassle him. She had not had that much to drink either, but still realised she should not be driving.

In custody, I did the formal breath test which proved her to be over the limit, but she also opted for a blood test. The blood test would take a little longer, as I had to wait for a nurse to come and administer the test. With the wait, I got on with doing the paperwork and all important arrest statements. I did offer to take her back to her car as it was now just after 5am and she would probably be below the limit. Before letting her get behind the wheel I did another quick breath test to check, and sure enough she was below the limit so she could at least get home.

At 6am, I got a rather curt and worried text from Mrs Hole, wondering where I had got to. By now I was feeling rather tired bearing in mind I had been up since just after 8am The drive home was difficult; I can see why they say that sleep deprivation is as bad as being drunk. Your mind does not work how it should and there have been sad cases of cops being killed on their way home, with the accident attributed to sleep deprivation. I drove home very carefully, I won't say I am the best of drivers anyhow, but tiredness really does not help. At 6:30am, I got home just in time to see my children wake up.

What was worse was that I had promised to take them to the zoo today for a family day out, so for their sakes did my best to say awake and only fell asleep in the car coming home. After making my wife do all the driving as I was not fit to drive.

Not long after this incident the 20% government cut's to police forces was announced. This would and has changed the way we police. Police force morale is at an all-time low and I cannot see it getting better anytime soon. With most police officers on a two year pay freeze, less staff and more work they feel that they have taken everyone's austerity measures.

Not long after the cuts were announced, my force announced its intention to close various smaller and underused police stations and contact points. My police station was one of those on the list. A few got sold off quite quickly as both the valuations and demand made it worthwhile. It was also a case of being able to find alternative accommodation for the move to take place.

In our case the valuation came in lower than expected, as it would really only be the land that was useable. The actual police station would be knocked down and the land reused possibly for housing. The next issue has been finding suitable alternative accommodation. The local parish council said no straight away due to lack of space. The local supermarket was unsuitable. The fire station is still a possibility but being a retained station the word is that it is not built to have people regularly in it?

Therefore, the search goes on, meanwhile as windows break, toilets break they are just covered in police tape and a "do not use sign" is placed over them. Our heating failed in the middle of winter and they were not going to fix it, but our Sergeant had a real go at management, as the heating was working fine until an engineer came into service it. No one knows if and when we will move, best thing is not to worry about it and continue. It will be a shame to move as the current station is very centralised and having us coming and going is a deterrent in itself.

However, with cuts you are left with some very hard choices. Over 200 cops have been either retired or left on medical grounds. Although the number that left on medical grounds was much smaller than the number forced to retire under A19. The thin blue line is now more of a thin blue dotted line. Quite a few cops have also been sacked in the past year for gross misconduct as the force cracks down hard on honesty and integrity. Which in itself is not a bad thing, but is further adding to the flow of cops leaving the job and shortage of manpower.

The Windsor report has further added insult to injury to cops, with most on a two year pay freeze. Then are seeing their salaries drop even further as various allowances are removed. Many people have little sympathy thinking that the police are already well paid and have gold plated pensions. The reality is that police officers are struggling to pay their bills, as the cost of living gets even more expensive. Teachers, firefighters and many other public servants are all in the same boat. There salaries are decent enough, but inflation and the cost of living is going up much faster than salaries. Many cops are having to do a second job, just make ends meet.

Here is a very candid account of what the Windsor report means to a frontline cop.

"Recent days and weeks have seen a campaign of spin, probably originating from Whitehall, aimed at draining public support for their police service. Yesterday saw a failed, sorry I mean ex–Chief Officer outlining how officers working on weekend get extra pay and that this should be cut.

As a Police Officer of 13 years myself, I would like to know which forces do pay their officers extra for working on weekends because I have not at that time have received a penny in extra allowances or 'perks' for working on weekends. Therefore, I would like a transfer please.

We have heard time and time again during these episodes of 'spin' that the police are not a special case and should be dealt with in line with all other public sector workers. Tell me this, which other public sector workers routinely put themselves in harm's way on a daily basis? Which other group are called to deal with the most depraved and anti-social of our communities? Which other group must routinely stand in a Crown Court and justify their actions in front of a judge and jury and constantly perform their duties with the cloud of discipline and/or prosecution hanging over them every minute of the day for mistakes or errors? Which other Public sector group will stand and defend the government (the very same government who seek to impose these cuts) during the inevitable demonstrations which will spring up when others of the public sector groups receive their cuts? Who will you call when you are assaulted or your house gets burgled or even when your neighbour plays their music too loudly?

Whilst you will be able to identify certain groups that perform one or perhaps two of the above actions, only one group performs them all: the police. The government and, in particular home secretary Teresa May, might wish to consider this when wielding their axe.

When she is being escorted home tonight by her armed police officer guards, who's pay and conditions she is seeking to cut, she might see fit to ponder who will be protecting her when those officers lose their jobs.

Yes, that's right. Front line police officer's jobs are going. Don't listen to the political dross spouting from politicians mouth in that front line jobs will not be affected. They are, every day!

The Tax Payers Alliance has recently identified that 700 of the 7,000 police officers in Wales are on 'restricted duties' i.e. unable to perform front line tasks. Even in the face of these figures, fully fit front line officers are losing their jobs through a clandestine police regulation called 'A19'. Not only are these officers fully fit they are the most experienced ones. Surely, the 700 restricted duties officer's positions should be more precarious than the fully fit ones? Next on the list of sticks with which to thrash the police is that of their pensions. Again, the campaign of 'spin' outlines how much the police receive from their retirement. Please let me clarify this. Serving police officers pay for the pensions of retired ones. It does not come out of government funds. The police pay 11% of their pay into those pensions which is far greater than any-one else in the Public sector, 6% being the nearest.

Again, the government has issued the threat that police pensions will be slashed. But in the process they totally neglect to mention the vast difference in the amounts that are paid in by officers.

I listened last week to the home secretary informing the nation that the police cannot strike and that she believed that very few officers would do so even if they could. On this point I strongly believe that Mrs May has underestimated the feelings of hatred that the police service now has for this government, which is in the process of betraying them so badly.

Can you just imagine what would happen if the police went on strike for just one hour? Businesses would have to shut up for fear of crime. Schools would have to close. Road accidents would go unattended as would all other crimes. The country would grind to a halt, the effects of which would cost millions and take far longer than 1 hour to recover from.

No appetite to strike on the part of the police? Nonsense, I would estimate that 80 -90% of officers would go out on strike. Perhaps the next time we see thousands of officers marching through Whitehall, the banner at the front of the march will read 'We Want the Right to STRIKE'.

Only a foolish government believes that it does not need the support of its police service, a government without the support of its police will undoubtedly fail. This is the situation that our government finds itself in at the moment. As the Police Federation has already said following the publication of Tom Windsor's report:

"WE ARE AT WAR"

It is a stark insight into how the average cop now feels. I can see exactly what they are talking about. I have noticed that there seem to be less and less cops on duty and at the same time I am responding and dealing with more incidents than I use to.

I remember coming on duty to go to an operation at a different station. I had just switched my radio on, when a call of an RTC involving a child just round the corner came in. Being so close I immediately said I would travel as the other cops had a six mile drive to get to me.

I quickly finished getting ready and threw my kit into the car and did the short quarter of a mile drive to the scene. The ambulance was already on scene and dealing with the casualty. A Ford C-Max was parked at the side of the road with a large dent in its bonnet, which made my heart race faster. As I got out I was greeted by the driver, who looked visibly shocked and quite pale.

I sat him in my car, as I wanted to find out about the state of the casualty so I could read it in. The girl who was about 10 was sitting up in the back of the Ambulance. She had been very lucky and suffered only minor cuts and bruises along with shock.

There was the annual village fair on this weekend and her mum had parked up to drop her off. Without thinking she had run round the back of the car and straight out in front of another car. Being a 30mph zone and the driver travelling below the speed limit the injuries had been very minor thankfully. When my full-time colleagues arrived they left me to it. Which as I said was a compliment that they trusted me to be able to sort it out. They simply got on with directing traffic and one cop who knew I would be stuck on an operation all night said he would fill out the accident card for me.

I finally got to my operation briefing, knowing what had happened the sergeant had waited for me to turn up. The operation was the usual burglary patrols, although with a fair with lots of teenagers in my area, in reality I should have been on duty there. The poor old response cops not on the operation got called out there, at least twice to disorder at the fair, whilst myself and the PCSO for the area was working in another area. If we had been there patrolling the disorder would probably not have taken place and stopped all the extra travelling, fuel and wasted time by other cops. It is back to this being more reactive than proactive, and the cuts have meant even more reactive stuff, almost done as a knee jerk reaction. At times it is like common sense thrown out of the window in terms of how resources are deployed and utilised. All this is down to lack of available manpower.

With the loss of cops from all areas of the organisation including response teams, cops are more stretched and their paperwork mountain has grown even higher. I can get sent to jobs in another area if I am deemed the only resource available or the closest resource. That distance could potentially be 25 miles to the edge of the force area on my side. We have been told to use our radios less and less as airtime costs money. With emphasis on using out Blackberrys to undertake checks on cars and people rather than use the radio. Crime numbers are no longer obtained over the air but we go back to the station and phone it through. Although one area that has helped is that they also fill out the crime report at the same time, which has saved paper and some writing time. Any cuts, no matter what the spin will affect the level of service. You cannot simply get rid of so called backroom jobs as someone still needs to undertake that task. All you can do is give those left behind more tasks and an extended workload which merely seems to increase the level of sickness and days off work.

We also have fewer vehicles than we had, which is not that bad for most inner city areas, but rural areas like ours need vehicles. Most of the roads are not really safe to cycle on being narrow 60mph roads. The vehicles we do have are well over the 100,000 mile change time some running into 150,000 miles and slowly falling apart.

Even though there is much moaning and griping from cops over the cuts and the current government. It has not hurt the professionalism I have seen from the cops that I work with. They still do an awful lot of goodwill and try to make sure the public has the service they deserve. For that, we should all be thankful and admire them, as never before has the service seen such cuts and so many changes including pay freezes. From the top to the bottom of the service everyone is trying their best to ensure the public is kept safe and we are still policing by consent.

Half the number of cops, now cover the same area, beat managers are on the verge of becoming more response orientated and PCSO's will be the beat team. As for specials that is still largely unknown. My force has strived for better trained specials, which leads me to think towards specials being expected to back fill response more and more. Maybe even allow some of them to be trained to respond with blue lights, which in some case would worry me greatly so I hope they filter out the ones who think a throttle is merely an on/off switch.

Forces have come to see specials as a resource or maybe for those more cynical cops, free labour that can fill the void of cops lost to retirement or resignation. Many forces want to double the number of specials over the next few years. But with that comes other issues. Whilst specials are indeed a good resource they do not receive the same level of training as a full time cop. Much of what they learn is on the job and due to the nature of how we work and what they do; often what they learn can be soon forgotten due to skill fade. A full-time cop still as to finish off an investigation, you cannot leave a suspect in the cells for a week waiting for the special to be next on duty.

I am glad to see that the force has recognised the need for better training for specials though. All new specials have up to two years with a regular officer and only after a year are they allowed to go out with other regular cops or experienced specials. This will mean the new breed of Specials will be much more competent and experienced. Retention should be much better as specials will feel much more integrated and better utilised. Some will always leave due to personal circumstances or it not being right for them. But then that is the same with any job. The idea is to raise the current two year average that most specials serve for. The final part has to be to reward experienced specials or those putting in plenty of hours with greater training opportunities. Be it being able to undertake riot training, or for those really keen to do the responsive driving course to be able to use blue lights. The final reward will be a quicker route into being a full-time cop and not having to go through virtually the same initial recruitment process and checks and a very similar application form. The bit a regular officer goes through that a special does not is the SEARCH assessment centre but with the NPIA gone, who knows what will happen to that in the long run?

In the end the recruitment process could certainly be made much easier for those with a proven ability be it a special or a PCSO. I would like see direct entry for those that have a proven track record and at least two years of competent service. A recommendation and reference along with a rigorous interview is all that should really be needed. The seven core competencies that are looked for in the recruitment process could easily be assessed "In the field" over a period of months and a decision made on the specials suitability to be a full-time officer. The whole idea of the core competencies is to assess someone against them to see if they have the aptitude and ability to be a cop. With at least two years' service, those same seven competencies will have been seen in a variety of situations if they parade on regularly and could in theory be marked off. Or the special is assessed over six months to see how many of the competencies they meet. Fall below and they will need to go through the application process score above and can progress without the assessment centre. I like many other cops may feel a little cheated though as we had to go through the full application process, but then I was not a special first and give up my time to serve the local community.

It would cut recruitment costs and possibly training costs. Many of these ideas are being discussed at a high level in preparation for when forces starting to recruit although some have started recruiting. Offering police officer recruitment to internal applicants only initially, so a step in the right direction. Some forces even offer training sessions or seminars to help internal applicants through the recruitment process which is not easy as over 70% of applicants are rejected at the application phase. Specials often score poorly as they try to show they are a good 'cop' rather than show how they meet the core competencies.

Jumper

I had just got myself all kitted up and ready to go for a 4pm start. I had a feeling that it was going to be one of those nights, don't ask me why, it was just a gut feeling. Preempting a busy night, I decided to go for an early tea and zapped my Chicken Korma for its full four minutes. Hoping that I would manage to eat it, such was my fear of being called to a job. There were other cops on duty, but all were busy and another area had five jobs stacking up. I managed to eat my Chicken Korma in record time without a call coming in

With a nice tummy full of curry, I made my way out on patrol for around 30 minutes, with the radio chattering away of jobs in other areas. One was a domestic that was unresourced and another, a PCSO had detained a male that had failed to appear in court on drug charges and was wanted, police speak of needing to be arrested. Finally, my peace and quiet was broken by the call of a high-risk missing person in my area. Her partner had rung in to say, his girlfriend had made off with £20 and 60 tablets for her various mental illnesses and was in quite a state. She had been in a bad way all day and was hearing voices in her head. I volunteered myself for the job as control had yet to realise I was on duty and available. Their screens have a list of available resources and often they do not actually realise you are available until you shout up for something. The control room is a hive of activity and a very busy place indeed. The course to become a control room operator is two weeks and quite intensive. As well as dealing with distraught members of the public they are undertaking background research be it PNC or checking other systems for info. Whilst tracking the various resources and taking updates from cops on the frontline, flicking between six or seven different systems and two computer systems. In many ways they are the unsung heroes of the police force, and get very little mention of the outstanding work they do.

When the call came in, I thought it would be just a local area search as I assumed she was on foot. Then an update came in to say she was in a car making it much harder to find her and a much wider search area. Other units were also sent but from other areas that were unfamiliar with my area and in need of directions. With the nature of the concern for safety, the woman potentially being suicidal and her existing issues it was classed as an immediate meaning blues and twos could be used. Luckily, I was already in the immediate area she had come from and started the initial search. Various updates were coming in, some contradictory as she had sent a text message to the off duty local beat manager saying where she was. I went to that location for an update to say she had now sent a text from a different location. The response sergeant jumped in to coordinate, and asked if they could locate her via her mobile phone by tracing it which is jargon for triangulating the phone's location. To locate the phone using multilateration of radio signals, it must emit at least the roaming signal to contact the next nearby antenna tower, but the process does not require an active call. GSM is based on the signal strength to nearby antenna masts and this is used to calculate the phone's actual position. The request to trace was denied initially, as is quite expensive to do and we are not quite CSi Miami! So the chase continued in almost a circuit of my area, with cars trying to vector in on the latest location update.

I always seemed to be on her tail by using local knowledge to make the best use of shortcuts, as various suggestions came in on where they thought she could be. She did reply to a couple of calls and all she said she was following her sat-nav and the voices in her head, before dropping the call and clearing the line. After she put the phone down for the third time, the officer speaking to her realised she was getting in a more and more distressed state, a mobile phone trace was finally authorised. The trace located her at a railway bridge right on the edge of my area and force area. I was third on the scene after a cop and three PCSO's. As I arrived, I could clearly see a person on the bridge with their legs dangling over. She had moved herself to over the river section as opposed the road. She was in a distressed state shouting out and rambling, the sight of more people caused her to become more agitated. Less the original cop on the scene, we backed off and got the road close as more cops arrived. Shortly followed by the British

Transport Police, being a railway it was their jurisdiction and needed to ensure the line was safe and clear. Being a freight line that is used mainly during the day, thankfully no more trains were due.

With six cops and three PCSO's already on the scene, next came armed response as they have advance first aid, followed by two fire engines. With all these vehicles on the scene, they parked up some distance away to ensure the female was not spooked any further. One end of the road was getting quite congested with emergency vehicles and it was thought best to widen the road block. The woman on the railway bridge who by now had a cop with her, was complaining about the amount of blue lights she could see so we had to turn them all off. With my vehicle, not being blocked in I was asked to drive a further half a mile down the road and block off the road. A further fire engine arrived on the other side of the bridge, followed half an hour later by a specialist team and a boat. By now, there were 30 firefighters and 20 cops and an ambulance on standby as and when required. A further two hours passed, with various updates including the arrival of two police negotiators. I just listened into 'Police FM' and a live episode of Police, Action without the camera to pass the time waiting for further updates. In simple terms sat and listened to my radio.

Two and a half hours after we had arrived, the radio burst out the words "she has jumped, she has jumped" My heart sank, as the fire brigade on standby jumped into action. They managed to pull the female out of the river within seconds of her having hit the water. They pulled her onto the bank still screaming and protesting. Quite an amazing feat, praise has to go to those guys for entering a swollen and very fast flowing river, putting themselves in harm's way to save life and limb. Two ambulances then raced to the scene one for the woman who had jumped, and the other for the firefighters who had been in the water. The female was unharmed, other than a bit wet and cold. She had been very lucky and the quick reactions by the fire brigade had saved her. Two of my colleagues escorted her to accident and emergency, before she was admitted into the mental health unit later on that night.

The resources needed for this incident were immense, cops had to be brought in from other areas to deal with any jobs coming in, whilst the local area cops were all tied up at the incident. When you talk about cuts to the emergency services and the amount of resources required to ensure one female is safe and well. Cut back on these essential services and you could say it is putting lives at risk. An operation like this needed a combined co-operation, the police to locate her, stop traffic and supply negotiators, the fire brigade to perform a rescue, the ambulance to deal with any injuries, notwithstanding the hospital and its staff needed to care for the woman once she was admitted. All of these are the same public services that the current government wants to cut.

Final thought and 2011 Riots

The riots of summer 2011 brought the police into media focus again. In many ways, the riots made people sit up and realise how much the police were needed. Facebook groups in support of the police popped up from all directions. Applications for Special Constables went up by about 50% although sadly the numbers did not swell by the same percentage as many of those that applied failed the security vetting procedure.

The riots were born out of boredom and frustration, along with the probable constant media coverage of cuts to the Police service, meaning the criminal element thought they could exploit it. Other factors include young people's dissatisfaction with the police and the over use of stop and search on certain ethnic minorities, are all factors thought to have been involved. Interestingly though, was that it all happened during the school holidays when youngsters were away from school or college. Maybe the shooting of Mark Druggen was just the trigger, which was then used as an excuse for wider disorder. Whatever the reason, police officers across the country came out onto the front line to protect life and property. The thin blue line did its very best to quell the disorder even though millions of pounds worth of damage, loss of life and injury were sustained.

I missed the riots completely as I was 2000 miles away on holiday, but received regular texts from my supervisors requesting me to come on duty. In the end my area did not suffer any disorder due to the riots. The force as a whole did an excellent job to quell any uprising, before it had a chance to start.

The lessons learnt; show just how much we all rely on the police in a time of need. It has not really stopped the government's cuts, nor what many cops believe to be a direct and sustained attack on the police by the current government. I am sure I will be adding an extra chapter in a couple of years of how everything panned out, and if the cuts were actually successful or not. All I know is that I am now much busier, and there are fewer cops to go round. Many cops want to get out and those that reach their 30 years of service are leaving rather than staying on. Some forces have lost up to 20% of their Police

Officers in the past few years due to A19, retirements and natural wastage. The hope that Specials would replace them has not panned out within many forces more leaving than can be recruited. With the Retention of Specials still running at around 40%. This leaves the front line quite sparse and many a stressed out and overworked cop. Recruitment has started in earnest across the country and hopefully this will ease the burden a little. But it takes around a year to recruit and fully train one police officer, so is not an instant fix.

Only last week I ended up going to a job out of the area, to support the other cops looking for what was classed as a high risk missing person. A man heavily in drink had been involved in a domestic incident with his wife and during the process hit his wife. So even though we had a concern for his safety we also wanted to arrest him for the assault if at all possible.

I knew the country park quite well after having taken my children and nieces there on several occasions. I had a PCSO and a good friend from my station with me and we chose a side entrance. The helicopter had just arrived overhead to do a wider area search. As this was quite an extensive park with many small tree copses and areas you could easily go to ground in if so desired. The park also has a heritage railway within it. After the helicopter had come up with nothing I said to the sergeant, I would check the railway station and rolling stock. As this was a great place to go to ground. I also got to re-kindle my childhood love of trains even if it was in the pitch black dark. Then went and tripped over a railway sleeper just missing the very oily locomotive bogie, which would have given me a lovely oil stain on my uniform. Boy do these old locomotives smell the stench of oil and diesel stayed up my nose for an hour or two. Oh yes back to the story, well the search of the station and rolling stock proved negative. We also decided to search the local roads around the park and that came up negative. At which time we were stood down and could go back to the Police station for tea, medals and home to bed. The man was found the next morning camping out in a wooded area of the park we had searched. But in the dark we would not have seen him, and only the helicopter with its thermal imaging camera had any chance of picking him out and that was also unable to see him.

On another busy Saturday night, with only two cops on duty, with the rest on leave, I was the lone ranger for the first time in quite a while. It was nice to be on my own for a change. I must admit though, it is nice to have someone else around to back you up or act as an 'extra' brain when mine fails to work quite as it should! It seemed initially, like it was going to be a quiet Saturday on my own just patrolling the area. There were very few young people about and even the roads seemed quieter than usual. Happily touring through a village my first call came in of a man wandering down a main road and at times wandering into the road in my area.

From the description given of his demeanour, I took a guess he had been drinking. Not being far away I made my way to the main road as another officer was dispatched on blue lights from 6 miles further away. Control had given us both and exact location, description, and I got there within 10 minutes of the call.

Both of us went up and down the road I even checked the local railway station and a village that fell just inside the adjoining force's area. The man had totally vanished who knows where he went; maybe he had been picked up, but was now nowhere to be seen. The minute I had finished my update to control, I was sent to the next job, which was at the supermarket two minutes down the road from the police station. Two males in their twenties had gone into the supermarket and had stolen two bottles of champagne along with some larger. Before they made their way out of the shop, only to be chased by two teenage shop assistants. Who managed to wrestle one bag away from one of the men, before the two men got away down a different street and then split up. I was second to arrive so started an area search whilst my colleague went to the shop to gather initial details and see if there was any CCTV.

By now, the local park had quite a few youths about and a few of the local lads, with their 'Halfords shop window' dressed Corsa that looked like it had ram raided the chrome accessories section. One of the lads was taking it to bits as he could not get into his glove box, maybe the glove was suffering under the strain of too much chrome!! Finally there was a 'Max power' Fiesta that was more Lax Power than Max Power complete with a 1.25 power house of an engine, that he said had a turbocharger. My guess is, he had just gaffa tapped his girlfriend's hairdryer to the air intake and then wired it up to the car battery.

Two of the lads standing next to Lax Power, did actually partially match the description and ages. Although I knew them well enough, that they would not to be daft enough to steal from a shop their regularly used surely not? I still double checked, and my initial thoughts that they were not involved proved true. I then talked to several groups that I knew and they all had seen these two males sitting on a bench at the park, and then later standing outside the local chip shop. But they had never seen them before in the village. One of the staff at the shop had seen them on a mobile as they were being chased. Most likely they had been picked up in a car and taken out of the local area. Most of the crime in the village and surrounding area, in particular burglary and theft, is nearly always committed by people who live some distance away. Often the next force area, then there is the saying that, "Criminals never shit on their own doorstep."

With that job completed, I went back for a nice cup of tea (you may have noticed I drink allot of tea) and just about to sit down to drink it. When I got yet another call to the same village, this time with reports of a twelve year old, who was threatening to hit several other teenagers over the head with a brick, as the group tried to calm him down. I tipped straight out to it and backup was on its way. Control upgraded the job to an immediate with me being single crewed and the potential for more serious violence. I quickly found the group and they denied seeing or hearing anything, so I carried on a little bit further and saw no one else. I span the car round and went back and questioned the group more directly. They admitted to seeing the lad and he had run off home up another street. They did not know where he lived, even though I suspect they probably did but I did get his name. I duly made my way back up the street he had just gone but to no avail, he too had vanished into the night like the lone male.

I made my way back to the group to gather more details and finally got to the truth. The lad had been angry about something or other, nobody seemed to know what. A couple of the girls had tried to calm him down and said he was being an, "Idiot" and told him to go home most probably on the sight of a police car coming down the road as I am sure he was twenty feet ahead of the group as I pulled up then disappeared. I went back for a final tour of the small housing estate and could not find him. Would have liked to of had a chat as it meant I could check there was no concern for safety, and checked off another box to keep the management happy. In the end all I could say that he had argued with a group, they had tried to calm him down and then sent him home. The reportee was a resident who had seen and heard the lad shouting in the road outside their house. With that I went back to have a nice cuppa before changing out of my 'glad rags' and making my way home after a busy but rewarding Saturday night.

My final story is an RTC I went to quite recently. I was with a PC Klingon, a real outdoors type who loved going on long treks. We were heading back to our station for tea and medals before going home, when we came across what looked like a scene of devastation and a serious RTC. We both looked at each other, before pulling up and getting stuck in. A post in the centre of the road, which was once an illuminated sign, was on its side and there was debris everywhere. A little further down the road there were two cars with people walking towards, as we tried to work out what had happened. I went to speak to the drivers, the first drive had hit the plastic bollard that had been left in the centre of the road but he had not hit the actual sign. In the process of hitting the bollard he had lost the plastic insert in the centre of the bumper of his Ford C-Max. The other driver had clipped the bent sign and scratched his wing, ripped off his wing mirror and hit a large chunk of tarmac strewn on the road causing him to suffer a blowout. Thankfully, no injuries, a kind member of the public had phoned and reported that a bollard was in the middle of the road just 5 minutes before we were on scene.

I did my bit by sweeping up the road and changing the elderly gentleman's front tyre, whilst my colleague went to see if the vehicle that had hit the sign was anywhere to be seen. We even had the police helicopter on standby, just in case the vehicle that had hit the sign had ended up in a nearby field with us being on a 60mph main country road. With nothing found and the type of impact, we both concluded it must have been a lorry. A car would have suffered serious damage and most likely un-drivable. Whatever had hit the sign had not stopped or even reported they had hit anything. They had just disappeared leaving debris everywhere, with a sign in a dangerous position and loose live electrical cables.

Highways arrived after about 20 minutes of control requesting them; a new all-time record. They got stuck in to make the sign safe so we could finally get back for more tea and medals. That is thing about police work, things are rarely what it seems and you never know what is lying around the corner.

I am proud to be a cop and proud to be able to make a difference no matter how small. I have made some good lifelong friends along with picking up some very useful life skills. I do have times when I cannot be bothered with it all and want to quit, but I have to admit if I take a short period of time off I actually miss not being on duty. Partly, as I miss the job, but also the people I work with that for some mad reason actually miss working with me. Which I suppose must mean I am either doing a good job or they miss my rather bad jokes!

I have always said, I will continue to be a cop until I lose the enthusiasm or the will to do it. That is of course if I still have a police force to work for as the cuts and changes reach their climax. Maybe the police force will be no more with private security firms such as G4S patrolling our streets? But then after the Olympics debacle, maybe they have shot themselves in the foot and shown why some services are better kept as a public service?

The Windsor report part I and II still has to take full effect, even if parts of it have been agreed and implemented already. All I know is that I have never seen cops so angry and so anti the government. They feel unjustly victimised and feel they have taken on most of the austerity measure alone. Cops may be able to retire early, but how many years can anyone deal with death and destruction on a daily basis? Deal with some of the most unpleasant people you are ever likely to meet and watch how badly people can treat each other. That is notwithstanding the numerous occasions that they are unable to get off duty, maybe 5 or 6 hours late due to dealing with an incident. Then not always getting paid overtime for it either, only the chance to maybe get off early another day.

There is a great amount of anger towards the current government and certain ministers for what has been allowed to happen. As time goes on I am sure more and more will come out of the woodwork, for the whole rationale, for what seems like a concerted effort to dismantle a public service. From inside and outside, it almost feels as if the police service is being victimised for something it has done wrong. Or maybe it is just the precursor to aid privatisation and companies like G4S waiting in the wings to move in.

As a cop, all I ask is that it stays a public service and I can stay as what I signed up to be, "A public servant" to prevent crime, investigate crime, reassure the public and be there in a time of need.

The face of crime is changing slowly, or should I say expanding with all these digital mediums that we have. Fraud is on the up, be it the traditional credit card type theft or identity theft. More and more crime is happening online through auction sites and even some big retailers. These offences can take place in a totally different location to where the IP lives. A good example is buying and selling on Ebay as this does now devour more and more police time. To curtail this new menace a national squad has been set up to reduce the workload on individual forces. With the grand name of Action Fraud here is the quote off the front page.

"We provide a central point of contact for information about fraud and financially motivated internet crime. If you've been scammed, ripped off or conned, there is something you can do about it - get in touch with us."

I had an hour long eLearning package to make my way through, in order to learn all about Action Fraud. It sounds like a good idea and even has some sound advice on how to avoid fraud in the first place. As sadly most of the time, fraud is driven by our desire for a bargain. Only last week Mr Mobile who owns a small mobile business replied to an advert on Gumtree for two iPhone 4s's at £200 each. The men involved wanted to meet up at a separate location, alarm bells should have rung at this point. But Mr Mobile decided he would go ahead but asked for the IME number of both phones.

"The IMEI number is used by a GSM network to identify valid devices and therefore can be used for stopping a stolen phone from accessing that network."

I got that quote that directly from Wikipedia how clever am I, or is that just good at being able to copy and paste, a bit like government inspectors…

Anyway back to the mobile phone story. The IME numbers checked out OK and Mr Mobile went to meet these men. He gave them £400 and in return he got two dummy cases with some lead weight inside. My advice is to try and avoid buying or selling second hand mobile phones over the internet, or through adverts. Better off recycling through a legitimate firm than selling, and as for buying then you may well be best off using Ebay, but never pay cash use PayPal. At least then if it goes wrong, as can be the case you have a chance of getting your money back.

Some sound advice from PC Hole, and an excuse to cut our workload slightly so we have more time to sit around eating doughnuts.

I will sign off with a classic police story that has been doing the rounds for years in one various form or another.

A woman phoned in with a report of what she thought was a man having sex with a woman on a flat balcony that she overlooked. Disgusted with what he was doing for everyone to see, she was also a little concerned that women appeared not to be moving almost as if she was drugged. Therefore, she decided to ring the police and due to the description and concern for safety, quite a few cars were sent including armed response. Local police were first on the scene and banged on the door. Looking through the slightly opaque door glazing, they could just make out someone making a stabbing action on what looked like a body on the floor. Armed response was called in, due to the potential of a knife or a weapon being present. They booted the door down to find a very red-faced man standing inside. Next to him lying on the floor was a deflated blow up doll with a knife. The same knife he had just used to quickly deflate the doll, on hearing police officers knocking on his door.

Just remember the police officer's motto, "In God we trust, all others are suspects."

When you ask a police officer round for tea, their four basic food groups are:

1. Glazed
2. Jelly
3. Powdered

4. Chocolate Frosted

Copyright

All rights reserved. No part of this publication may be reproduced, stored in a retrieval system, or transmitted, in any form or by any means, electronic, mechanical, photocopying, recording or otherwise, without the prior permission of the publishers. This is a work of fiction and does not relate to or represent any UK police force. Any connection to any real person or location is purely coincidental and unintentional.

Copyright 2012 © Andrew Hole
ISBN: 978-1-291-65274-1

Printed in Great Britain
by Amazon.co.uk, Ltd.,
Marston Gate.